MW01079683

Odenville Public Library

Jesus

and

You

Discovering the Gospel in Everyday Living

Joey Rich

JOEY RICH

Odenville Public Library
P O Box 249
Odenville, AL 35120

Walmart, Jesus and You
Copyright 2013 by Joey Rich
All rights reserved

No part of this publication may be used or reproduced in any manner without written permission except in case of brief quotations embodied in articles and reviews.

ISBN-13:978-1482683936
ISBN-10:1482683938
Also available in eBook

Cover and Interior Book Design:
Ellen C. Maze, The Author's Mentor, www.theauthorsmentor.com

Unless otherwise indicated, Scripture quotations used in this book are taken from The New King James Version, © 1979,1980,1982 by Thomas Nelson, Inc. Publishers. Used by permission. All rights reserved.

Other Scripture quotations are from the following:
Scripture quotations identified (KJV) are from *The Holy Bible*, King James Version
Scripture quotations identified (MSG) are from *The Message*. Copyright © 1993, 1994, 1995, 1996, 2000, 2001, 2002. Used by permission of NavPress Publishing Group."
Scripture quotations identified (NIV) are from THE HOLY BIBLE, NEW INTERNATIONAL VERSION®, NIV® Copyright © 1973, 1978, 1984, 2011 by Biblica, Inc.™ Used by permission. All rights reserved worldwide.

Scripture quotations marked (NLT) are taken from the Holy Bible, New Living Translation, copyright © 1996, 2004, 2007 by Tyndale House Foundation. Used by permission of Tyndale House Publishers, Inc., Carol Stream, Illinois 60188. All rights reserved.

Scripture quotations marked (HCSB) are taken from the Holman Christian Standard Bible®, Copyright © 1999, 2000, 2002, 2003, 2009 by Holman Bible Publishers. Used by permission. Holman Christian Standard Bible®, Holman CSB®, and HCSB® are federally registered trademarks of Holman Bible Publishers.

Scripture quotations marked (NASB) are taken from the NEW AMERICAN STANDARD BIBLE®, Copyright © 1960,1962,1963,1968,1971,1972,1973,1975,1977,1995 by The Lockman Foundation. Used by permission.

PUBLISHED IN THE UNITED STATES OF AMERICA

To my wife, Donna.
My love, my life, my encourager.
Without your patience, your suggestions, your editing
and your prayers,
this book would not exist.

Who can find a virtuous wife?
For her worth is far above rubies.
The heart of her husband safely trusts her;
So he will have no lack of gain.
Proverbs 31: 10-11 NKJ

Table of Contents

Acknowledgments

To acknowledge everyone that has made this book possible would be impossible. As a novice, I have asked various questions and advice from so many individuals. So to all the folks that helped but are not mentioned in this acknowledgment, I sincerely thank you. The Lord knows who you are and may He richly bless you.

However, there are some people that have helped birth this book that I must mention out of gratitude for all they have done. First of all, I want to acknowledge and thank my wife, Donna. She has helped, directed, edited, suggested, and encouraged me more than anyone else. Without her, this book would not exist. When I was overwhelmed with the task, she would get me back on track. When I would fall back into the habit of writing in a business style, she would say, "Remember, you are painting a picture," or "You have to make it flow." In reality, Donna has co-authored this book, but she would not allow me to recognize her as such. To her, "Thank You and I love you" seem so inadequate.

For Joey Jr. taking time from his busy schedule and looking at those rough drafts, I am deeply grateful. With his writing skills, I am sure he would be successful writing his own book.

Words cannot express my gratitude to Denise George, author of over 27 books and more than 1500 articles. The Boot Camp for Christian Writers founded by Denise, along with Carolyn Tomlin, was invaluable to me. But my appreciation is not limited to the seminars. As an amateur, I had so many

2

questions for Denise, and she answered every one with the patience of a teacher and authority of the professional author that she is. Denise, may God continue to bless every Boot Camp seminar, and may your legacy live through the Boot Campers you train.

I also owe a sincere thank-you to Nina Lockard, who edited the book. I didn't realize how many errors I had made until Nina pointed them out. The grammar, punctuation, etc. was way over my head. Her suggestions and corrections have made this book much more readable. The task was difficult, but she never complained and was a joy to work with.

In addition, I must express my gratitude to Ellen C. Maze, author, book designer and founder of "The Author's Mentor." I was amazed at her ability to look at the typed pages and describe the possibilities that she envisioned in my book. The beautiful cover of this book is a small example of the creativeness and artistic resourcefulness that God has gifted her with. Anyone can tell that helping new and inexperienced writers become published authors is not a job – it is a ministry for Ellen.

Finally, I must mention the One who should receive all the glory (I Corinthians 10:31). I realize my opportunity and attempt as an amateur writer was only possible by the grace of God. Through this book, may He challenge others to discover the Gospel in everyday living and inspire others much more qualified than I, to write better books than this to explain and teach the wonderful truth of God's Word in our everyday living.

About the Author

Being raised in the small rural community of Prescott, Alabama and having parents with only a sixth grade education provided Joey with an education that very few have the opportunity to experience. With a strong Christian mother, the Bible became alive as she lived her life. Meanwhile, an honorable work ethic was instilled by a dad that usually had two jobs.

Growing up with all the wonders of nature, one grandmother that was raised in an orphanage and the other a mother of ten, one granddad that was illiterate and the other a blacksmith, and a community that had an abundance of "characters," there was never a shortage of storytelling and activities.

Joey earned a B.S. from the University of Alabama in Birmingham and a M.A. in Christian Education from New Orleans Baptist Theological Seminary. He has served Alabama churches as minister of education and bi-vocational pastor. In 2010, he was the recipient of the Troy L. Morrison Award as Bi-vocational Pastor of the Year in the Alabama Baptist State Convention. In addition to serving in churches, Joey is a successful businessman and entrepreneur.

He and his wife, Donna, have been married for forty-two years and have two grown sons – Joey Jr. and his wife Emily who are expecting a baby girl and Matt and his wife Sarah who have a son Micah.

Proceeds from the sale of this book will go to assist with Southern Baptist international missions efforts through the Lottie Moon Christmas Offering®.

Preface

As I grow older, the simplicity of the gospel of Jesus Christ becomes more and more evident to me. Throughout the Bible, we find stories of everyday people, going about living their lives and while they are doing this, the wonderful gospel is presented. For example, a shepherd watching sheep glorifies God as the Great Shepherd, who makes us to lie down in green pastures and leads us besides the still waters.

Today is no different. Within this book, a trip to Walmart, my wife's car wreck caused by a buzzard, children, a pile of junk, getting lost on vacation, ordering a hamburger, frustration with computers, a mother's love for her child, memories, a favorite relative, a physical injury, a western movie, electronics, parents, accounting and personal trials will allow you to see the gospel in some of the true, personal events in my life.

As you laugh and identify with many of the experiences that begin each chapter, you will then read what Jesus and additional scriptures have to say about the experiences. Each chapter has a different topic. For instance, when Jesus' teaching about plans are laid alongside a trip to Walmart, it helps us to understand why plans are changed and how to apply the biblical principle concerning the change of plans to our lives. With each chapter, you will begin to learn how the gospel is found in everyday living and begin to read the Bible as commentary and direction for your own life.

With each theme being identified in the Table of Contents, and a list of Bible verses and references used located in the back of the book, *Walmart, Jesus and You* becomes a book that is to be referred to again and again.

Chapter 1: Walmart, Jesus and You

"Mortals make elaborate plans, but God has the last word." ~Proverbs 16:1 MSG

Have you ever had a simple shopping trip turn into a complicated mess? Have you ever grabbed a shopping cart only to find it has a bad wheel? Do the terms "I need a price check" or "I'm sorry, we are out of that item" sound familiar to you? If so, this first chapter is especially for you.

Walmart

Before I begin, I want to point out my opinion concerning a few distinct characteristics between a shopper and a customer. Shoppers are a breed of their own. Shopping is their calling. A shopper may spend hours going from aisle to aisle searching for a great sale item. At other times, they might not know what they are looking for, but they know if they shop long enough, they will find the treasure that others have overlooked. Typically, the store will make very little profit from a shopper. On the other hand, customers know what they want before they go to the store. The customer wants to get in and get out. And the price is not as important to the customer as it is to the shopper. Woe unto the store that has more shoppers than customers and blessed is the store with more customers than shoppers.

Certainly there are other differences, but just these few differences provide enough evidence to find me "not guilty" of being a shopper. Even if I did want to be a shopper, I wouldn't have a chance against the "professionals." You know the ones I'm talking about.

For instance, survival has made the young mom with a baby in a papoose, a toddler in the cart, and a three year old walking alongside her, a professional shopper. Not enough money for the number of mouths to feed makes shopping an act of financial survival. Not only is financial survival at risk, but mental survival is too. If she doesn't get out of the house and shop, she will not survive. Depending on various factors such as body weight, hydration, and health in general, a strong person can survive a month or more without food. I estimate a mom with three or more toddlers less than four years old can only survive mentally about a month at the most without going shopping. This can be less depending on potty training, number of hours the husband works, etc. Warning - don't even think about getting in the way of this young mother shopper.

Then there is the shopper I will call "the coupon lady." As she stands in front of her cart guarding her position in front of the soups, she looks at each coupon in order to save $1.00 on ten cans. But don't move her cart or ask her to please excuse you – she is doing some serious mathematics. Just go on by and come back in 20 minutes.

Before I go any further, I want to make it clear that the male species of the shopper can be just as bad, if not worse, than the female species. The male shopper tends to gather in groups or in pairs. For example, often you will find two or three male shoppers in the middle of an aisle in the sporting goods department. All have empty shopping carts and are in a thirty-minute conversation about their great golf game or fishing trip or hunting trip. Don't try to go down that aisle – you will never get through. In my mind, I can see the "do not enter" red tape at both ends of the aisle.

Another reason I couldn't be a professional shopper is because of all the missing children in the store. Yet, it seems not to bother the professional shopper. Have you ever noticed how many children go missing in stores? "Jimmie Jones, your mom is at the front of the store. Please come to the front." Five minutes later, the announcement is repeated. "Jimmie Jones, your mom is at the front of the store. Please come to the front." All the announcements of lost children don't slow down the professional shopper. When I hear such an announcement, I fear the worst for the child. The person on the PA system needs to go look for Jimmie. Could it be possible that Jimmie has been claimed by the lady with the papoose? After an hour or more with her clan, she probably doesn't know who she is or who belongs to her. If not with her, then Jimmie could have gotten in the way of the coupon lady. For that reason, she hit him in the head with a can of soup. Jimmie is laid out cold on aisle four. Or it could be that he entered the "red tape" area and the man with the biggest fish story is convinced that Jimmie needs to hear his story. "Son, come here, let me tell you about ..."

If it does become necessary for me to purchase something, I am a customer, not a shopper. I try to avoid any of the aforementioned "hurdles" by having everything planned out in my mind before I get there. Usually the trip is based on a need, certainly not for the joy of the trip. So before I go I know what I want to purchase. Then, with a little planning, I should be in and out in a matter of 10-15 minutes. Mission accomplished.

For example, if I should need a new outdoor lounge chair, I can go on the Internet and see what is available at the local stores. After I find the one I like, I plan my trip with great detail. First, never try to park close to the doors. Leave those places to the handicap or elderly who deserve it or to the lazy bums that don't deserve it. Park about half way down the parking lot and then walk to the store (which is good exercise). Enter via the garden center entrance where there is less traffic. Grab a cart and go directly to where the chair is located. Put it in the cart and go to the check-out register in the garden center. Pay, get to the car, and go home. The plan is very simple. Only one problem, it never works out the way I plan it!

My plan starts to fall apart when I arrive in the parking lot. I find carts in my way or huge freight trucks filling both sides of the parking space. No problem. I need to walk, so I park in a space at the end of the lane. As I enter the store, a nice lady greets me with a smile and the parking problem is forgotten. I grab a cart and continue with my plan. As I push the cart, I notice I have selected a cart that has a bouncing wheel and making all kinds of noise. No problem. I'll just be in and out. I go to the area to pick up the item but find that there was a limited supply and it is now sold out. My brain is telling me to refuse to accept defeat and simply look at another chair. Only a few dollars difference over the life of the chair would be pennies a week. Therefore, the only logical thing to do is to purchase another chair. So I select the substitute and place it in the cart. As I push my bouncing cart to the checkout lane, I find to my surprise and my delay, a lady has decided to use the garden register to check out her entire grocery list. No problem, she only has about twelve items left. Then, with only four items left, I hear those infamous words, "Marge, we need a price check in the garden center." After four minutes and seventeen seconds (but who is really counting?), the price is confirmed and the lady goes her way. By this time, the clerk at the register is ready for a person with one item, and I am glad to be that person. Finally, I smile to the nice lady at the door and head for the car. After walking to the end of the parking lot, I find a shopping cart pushed against my car – so much for my great plan.

Jesus

The older I get, the more I realize my life is like my trip to Walmart. Often my plans get changed by God, and I am thankful He does. Other times my hard head thinks I know best, and I end up with a mess that requires a change in plans. I think everyone has had their plans changed at one time or another in their life.

Our plan versus God's plan is nothing new. Abraham and Sarah had everything planned. Since Abraham and Sarah assumed Sarah could not have children, they had a plan to provide Abraham with an heir. The only problem was that God had a different plan.

In chapter 22 of the book of Jeremiah, we find God telling self-centered and arrogant King Jehoiakim that sorrow awaited him instead of all his wonderful plans of having a great palace and a kingdom that glorified him.

> And the LORD says, "What sorrow awaits Jehoiakim, who builds his palace with forced labor. He builds injustice into its walls, for he makes his neighbors work for nothing. He does not pay them for their labor. He says, 'I will build a magnificent palace with huge rooms and many windows. I will panel it throughout with fragrant cedar and paint it a lovely red' " (Jeremiah 22:13-14 NLT).

> Therefore, this is what the LORD says about Jehoiakim, son of King Josiah:..."It may be nice to

live in a beautiful palace paneled with wood from the cedars of Lebanon, but soon you will groan with pangs of anguish—anguish like that of a woman in labor" (Jeremiah 22:18a, 23 NLT).

Notice the statement "I will." But the plans of King Jehoiakim failed. God foretold what was to happen to Jehoiakim. "He shall be buried with the burial of a donkey, dragged and cast out beyond the gates of Jerusalem" (Jeremiah 22:19).

Our plan versus God's plan was a problem in Jesus' day. In chapter 12 of the book of Luke, Jesus told the parable of the rich fool who makes all his plans to build bigger barns, and store his crops. Then he was going to "eat, drink and be merry" for many years. "But God said to him, 'Fool! This night your soul will be required of you' " (Luke 12:20a).

As I read about Jehoiakim and the rich fool, I thought about how foolish they were. Then I thought about how I would plan a trip to Walmart and find the same mindset. Words like "I" and "my" were scattered throughout my planned trip. I realized that not only did the rich man and Jehoikim have a self-centered attitude, I did too. How self-centered to think I could get upset over a change in my plans to purchase something I need. "I need?" How ridiculous! People need to know the love of our Lord. People need clean water, food, medical attention, freedom from persecution and so much more. But to use the word "need" concerning a lounge chair is self-centeredness to the core. There is a great deal of difference between want and need. A Christian family fleeing persecution, trying to walk a hundred miles to a refugee camp has a need. A new lounge chair is not a need. I need a change/transformation of my mind. Vance Havner (considered by many to be the most quoted minister of the 20th century) once said, "We cannot change our hearts, but we can change our minds; and when we change our minds, God will change our hearts."[1]

Sometimes plans need to be changed not because they are self-centered or that we are a rich fool but simply because God has a different purpose for our lives. Moses seemed to be perfectly content being a shepherd the rest of his life. After all, he had tried to free the Israelites (his way—one at a time) and it didn't work. He ran and became a shepherd, but God had a different plan for his life.

In the New Testament we find Jesus changing people's plans. Peter's plans are changed when Jesus said, "Come, follow me." Saul's plans are changed on the road to Damascus. Others would include Andrew, Matthew, Pricilla and Aquilla, James and John, just to mention a few.

Looking back, we all have had plans that have been changed. We all have had to park at the end of the lot. Maybe not at the end of a literal parking lot, but maybe we had to take a job that wasn't what we expected. We all have grabbed a cart with a bad wheel. Maybe not a literal cart, but a divorce or sickness that was unexpected. We all have gone to purchase an item and it was out of stock. Maybe not a literal item, but a friend that you thought would always be there but wasn't when you needed them most. We all have gone to the wrong check-out counter. Maybe not a literal counter, but someone was blocking our way. You wanted to move on but the legal system made you wait. All of us have had our plans changed. The one difference is as Christians we can be assured that if our plans are changed then God is changing them for our good. In the Bible, God gives us this promise: "For I know the plans I have for you," declares the Lord. "Plans to prosper you and not to harm you, plans to give you hope and a future" (Jeremiah 29:11 NIV).

You

This is not really about Walmart. We all have experienced things that can happen there or at Target or Macy's or any other store. It is not really about Jesus. He has made His voice very clear about our plans. He simply says to trust Him. The true area of focus is you.

In life, all of us will experience times when the status quo is not an option. Change is inevitable. When changes in your plans are necessary, you will have to make a decision concerning where you place your trust. The following story shared by Ron Mehl will help understanding this certainty.

> An old sea captain named Eleazar Hall lived in Bedford, Massachusetts, during the time of the great sailing ships. He was renowned, legendary, and revered as the most successful of all sea captains of the day. He worked harder, stayed out longer, and lost fewer men while catching more fish than anyone else.
>
> Captain Hall was often asked about his uncanny ability to stay out so long without navigational equipment. He'd once been gone for two years without coming home for a point of reference.
>
> Eleazar simply replied, "Oh, I just go up on the deck and listen to the wind and rigging. I get the drift of the sea, look up at the stars, and then set my course."
>
> Well, times changed in Bedford. The big insurance companies moved in and said they no longer insure the ships if the captains didn't have a certified and properly trained navigator on board. They were terrified to tell Eleazar. But to their amazement he said, "If I must, I will go and take the navigational courses."
>
> Eleazar graduated high in his class, and having greatly missed the sea, he immediately took off for a long voyage. On the day of his return, the whole town turned out to ask him the question:

"Eleazar, how was it having to navigate with all those charts and equations?"

Eleazar sat back and let out a long, low whistle. "Oh," he replied, "it was simple. Whenever I wanted to know my location, I'd go to my cabin, get out my charts and tables, work the equations and set my course with scientific precision. Then I'd go up on the deck and listen to the wind and rigging, get the drift of the sea, look at the stars, and go back and correct the errors that I had made in computation."

When I heard that, I prayed, *Lord, I want to know You that way. I want to go up on deck, hear Your quiet voice in my heart, consider Your eternal Word, and then go back down below and make adjustments to all those fine, logical, scientific plans I've drawn up in my head.*[2]

Walmart, Jesus and You. I pray you will "make adjustments to all those fine, logical, scientific plans" you have made and put yourself in the hands of the One that does not change. Your plans or God's plans? Which will it be?

Chapter 2: Buzzards, Jesus and You

"May God raise up a people who will consult their pleasures less and the great need more."[1]

Buzzards

In 2012, Donna and I celebrated our 42nd anniversary. During this time, we have come to know and experience Ecclesiastes 3:1. It is very true that "to everything there is a season, and a time to every purpose under the heaven." But what I am about to tell you is a time of "I can't believe it." But it is true!! It happened to us!!

One Sunday morning I talked Donna into driving to church. The reasons are very simple. I'm not crazy about driving. It can be very boring and seems a waste of time. Also, I am not a morning person. At that time she drove a big SUV. She loves a large vehicle because it makes her feel safer. Honestly, I believe only parking decks prevent her from driving a freight truck. Her motto is "the bigger, the better."

Traveling in the SUV, we left our home in Prescott, Alabama, and headed east on old Highway 78 through Cook Springs toward I-20. For those not familiar with the area, the road is straight, then goes under a railroad trestle and makes a couple of turns. On that particular morning, as we headed into the straightaway, I looked up from my half-asleep world and saw this big bird in the road. As we got closer, I could see it was a buzzard enjoying his morning meal, and he was right in the middle of Donna's lane. Now Donna is an excellent driver, but I noticed the buzzard wasn't moving, and the steering wheel wasn't either. I looked at Donna, and I looked at the buzzard. By then I was wide-awake and realized traveling 50 mph toward a huge bird is not good. Suddenly, the buzzard looked up and tried to take off with a big hop. The hop got him about two feet in the air and –BAM! – right into the grille of the SUV he went. I said (in a loving manner), "You hit that buzzard – didn't you see that buzzard?!" No response. Just in case she didn't hear me, I repeated, "You hit that buzzard – didn't you see that buzzard?!" She replied, "I thought he would move, and he was in my lane." I said, "Pull over, pull over!! I've got to look at the damage!!" She pulled over, and I got out to survey the damage. As I went around to the front of the SUV, the feathers confirmed that the buzzard had eaten his last meal. Then I saw this big, stinking, ugly buzzard embedded in the grille of the SUV. Recognizing that it would cause too many questions for a minister to be riding in his wife's vehicle with a buzzard embedded in the grille, I had no other option than to remove it. I grabbed the end of one wing and pulled. Realizing I wasn't getting the job done, I pulled harder and harder. Then, like an accordion, the wing came out… then the body …then the other wing. The buzzard was huge and there was no way I could throw it off the road. So, holding onto the bird, I turned around like a discus thrower, hurling the bird as far as I could. With the buzzard removed from the grille, I could see major damage to the SUV. I got back in and with total disbelief said, "I can't believe you hit that buzzard!" Silence. Again, "I can't believe you hit that buzzard!!" This time I added, "I have never heard of anyone hitting a buzzard!" Her reply was short and simple. "YOU

18

wanted me to drive. YOU should have driven!" Well, now it was MY fault! She then asked me if I wanted to go on to church or go back to the house. I decided we should continue on - it was the only "Christian" thing to do. As a precaution, I turned off the air conditioner and began to watch the temperature gauge. To help get the feel of dead buzzard off my hands, I reached into the console for hand disinfectant and some paper towels. We went about a quarter of a mile under the railroad and around a curve. All of a sudden, as I am cleaning my hands, I got jerked from one side to the other. I looked up and saw nothing. I asked, "What in the world is going on?" She replied. "Didn't you see that little squirrel in the road?" I said, "A squirrel? You just hit a huge buzzard and now you are dodging a little squirrel? You can hit a squirrel! It's okay!!" Needless to say, it was a very, very, long and quiet trip to church.

However, there is justice in the world. Donna had to go to the various body shops and get estimates for the repair. Most of the comments from the body shops were "Looks like you hit a deer." Donna, honest about the accident, would say, "No sir, not a deer - a buzzard." I can only imagine the smiles on their faces.

For the record, I did apologize for my attitude and got permission to use this. I, myself, have done a lot worse. Thank you, my love.

Jesus

You may laugh and think that really didn't happen. It really did. But hitting buzzards and dodging squirrels is nothing new. Throughout history people have been doing this. It was so prevalent in Jesus' day that He actually addressed the issue. For example, notice the following verses from chapter

23 of the Gospel of Matthew concerning squirrels and buzzards.

> Woe to you, scribes and Pharisees, hypocrites! For you pay tithe of mint and anise and cumin, and have neglected the weightier matters of the law: justice and mercy and faith. These you ought to have done, without leaving the others undone. Blind guides, who strain out a gnat, and swallow a camel! (Matthew 23:23-24).

I am sure you noticed Jesus talking about what the scribes and Pharisees were doing and what they were not doing. But did you notice the part about the squirrels and buzzards?

If you didn't, I would like to give you some definitions/explanations and then paraphrase the verses.

> *"Woe to you"* is a term that could mean "how awful, how dreadful, how terrible, or how horrible it will be to you."
>
> *"Scribes and Pharisees"* were the religious leaders in that time.
>
> *"Tithe"* according to Numbers 18:20-24, required a Jew to devote a tenth part of all to the tribe of Levi for their service in the Tabernacle.
>
> *"Mint, anise and cumin"* were herbs that were of little worth.
>
> *"Weightier matters"* were matters of importance.
>
> *"Law, judgment, mercy, and faith"* were important matters in our relationship to God and man.
>
> *"Gnat"* is a very small animal.
>
> *"Camel"* is a very large animal.

By substituting some of the definitions above, verses 23 and 24 could read as follows: (Please remember, this is a paraphrase not a translation. I just want you to see the squirrels and the buzzards in these verses.)

> How horrible, how dreadful, it will be to you
> religious leaders that are nothing but hypocrites!
> You pay great attention to giving a tenth of your
> herbs that have little value, but you ignore the
> important matters in your relationship to God
> and man: You blind guides!! You are hitting
> buzzards and dodging squirrels.

In other words, the religious leaders paid a lot of attention to the little things, the unimportant things in life, but paid no attention to the big things, the important things in life.

It is easy to agree with Jesus and point our religious finger at those hypocrites in the first century. But before we do, we should remember Jesus was not just talking to them, but to us as well. Today, the warning is still about ignoring important matters in our life, while at the same time, placing great importance on the unimportant things in life.

However, at times, it is difficult to make a distinction between the unimportant and the important. A. W. Tozer, author of more than 40 Christian books, wrote: "Life as we know it in our painfully intricate civilization can be deadly unless we learn to distinguish the things that matter from those that do not."[2]

When we die – not "if" but "when," and if we could look back at our life, it would be very easy to tell what was important and what was not important. As one person has said, "When the film of our lives is shown, will it be as great as it might be? A lot will depend on the multitude of 'good' things we need to eliminate to make way for the great things God wants to do through us."[3] I realize as we live our lives it can be confusing to differentiate between the important and the unimportant. Maybe a look at the squirrels and the buzzards will help.

All squirrels (the unimportant things in life) are classified as "self squirrels." The name is based on the fact that one's life is determined by what the self wants. There are many subclasses of "self squirrels." There is the beauty squirrel, the physical fitness squirrel, the workaholic squirrel, the computer squirrel, the couch potato squirrel, the keeping up with the Joneses squirrel, the power squirrel, the addiction squirrel, which includes drugs, alcohol, and pornography, and the domineering squirrel. These are just a few of the subclasses of "self squirrels." No one wants to hit any of these squirrels. That would mean death to what self wants.

All buzzards (the important things in life) are "relational buzzards." The name is based on the fact that one's life is determined by relationships. There are many subclasses of "relational buzzards." Unlike the "self squirrels," the "relational buzzards" are harder to identify. A few examples would be the marital buzzard, the family buzzard, and the church buzzard. Although there are millions of strong marital, family and church buzzards, the number of these subclasses is being threatened at an increasing rate. They all are endangered in many ways. For example, the marital buzzard is endangered when a marriage is falling apart or when a divorce is getting closer and there will be major consequences that will affect children, holidays, and life in general. The family buzzard is threatened when a daughter or son will barely speak to their parents or when relationships with other family members are crashing like waves hitting the rocks. The church buzzard is endangered and becomes weak when jealousy, disharmony and confusion are found in the church.

In life, you may not experience any of the squirrels or

buzzards mentioned above. Your squirrel or buzzard may be some other subclass not mentioned. But there is one buzzard that everyone will encounter on their road of life and that is the spiritual buzzard. The spiritual buzzard always involves God. It may be God dealing with a believer whose relationship with Him has grown cold. It may be God calling a person to a particular area of service. But the most important spiritual buzzard of all is the salvation buzzard. If this buzzard is ignored, the results will have eternal consequences. A. W. Tozer wrote:

> This is so desperately a matter of importance for every human being who comes into the world that I first become indignant, and then I become sad, when I try to give spiritual counsel to a person who looks me in the eye and tells me: "Well, I am trying to make up my mind if I should accept Christ or not."

> Such a person gives absolutely no indication that he realizes he is talking about the most important decision he can make in his lifetime.[4]

Of all the buzzards (things of importance), the salvation buzzard is the greatest buzzard of them all. This relational buzzard will determine where a person spends eternity. Some will ignore this buzzard and rationalize that this buzzard does not matter because everyone will go to heaven. As Vance Haver once said, "Our Savior has gone to prepare a place, but there are places only for those who make reservations. The dying thief made a reservation: 'Remember me.'"[5]

You

Speaking of squirrels and buzzards, I want to make one thing very clear. There is certainly nothing wrong with dodging squirrels. There is nothing wrong with working hard or providing for your family, or keeping physically fit, or knowing all the facts about your favorite team. What *is* wrong is paying a lot of attention to squirrels and at the same time ignoring the buzzards in your life.

You may be making sure the kids are going to ball practice. You are a member of the hunting club or the golf club. You are busy with the local activities. You even attend church religiously. You have been really good at putting emphasis on all these little squirrels. Everybody looks at you and thinks you have it all together. But you know your life is a wreck with dented fenders, broken headlights and a crushed grilled. You know it is a wreck because you have hit one or two buzzards before. You have tried to fix your wreck. Yet, it seems, everything you have tried has destroyed and robbed you of a meaningful life. You just exist. You need help. You need someone that knows how to fix your wreck. That person is Jesus.

Jesus speaks to all of us who have hit buzzards when He says, "Come to Me, all you who labor and are heavy laden, and I will give you rest" (Matthew 11:28). In other words, "Come unto Me, all of you wrecks, and I will fix you." However, it is sad to say that there are so many people who know they are a wreck and know whom to go to - but refuse to go. The more they drive or try to continue, their condition gets worse and worse. They continue to do the same thing and expect a different result. Are you one of those individuals? If you are, aren't you tired of being a wreck?

John Newton, the author of "Amazing Grace," came to a

point in his life where he realized that his life was a wreck – not just a fender bender, he had totaled his life. None of us can probably compare to his wreck, but he realized it. Newton wrote his own epitaph which reads, "John Newton, Clerk, once an infidel and libertine, a servant of slaves in Africa, was, by the rich mercy of our Lord and Savior Jesus Christ, preserved, restored, pardoned, and appointed to preach the faith he had long labored to destroy." After becoming a believer he wrote, "Amazing grace, how sweet the sound that saved a wretch like me."

We have all wrecked (Romans 3:23). We deserve to be scrapped and thrown into the furnace (Romans 6:23). The difference is some wrecks, like me, have realized and admitted that we were wrecks. As a result, we did something. We went to Jesus. We trusted Him as our personal Savior and by faith we believed and called on Him to save us (Romans 10:13). Jesus died on Calvary not just to repair us but to make us new (II Corinthians 5:17). He can do the same for you. Then you can sing, "Amazing grace how sweet the sound that saved a *wreck* like me."

Today, everyone is on a highway. It is not Highway 78, but it is the highway called life. You may be looking down the road and see a buzzard – not a physical buzzard, but it is a big buzzard – in fact, the biggest. You think or hope the buzzard is going to move, so you just continue to drive, living life the same as you always have. The buzzard will not move. The buzzard is death. When you hit this buzzard – and you will – your relationship with Christ will determine where you spent eternity. After death there is no "getting it fixed." It will be too late. However, the wonderful news is if you're reading this, it is not too late.

Jesus, buzzards, but what about you? Are you looking down the highway and seeing a buzzard in your lane? What are you going to do?

Chapter 3: Lewers Street, Jesus and You

"If you don't know where you're going, you will wind up somewhere else."[1]

Lewers Street

I am sure none of you have the same problem that I have. My wife Donna and my sons, Joey Jr. and Matt, have no problem with it. If you do and admit it, you are an exception rather than the rule. My problem is simple. I'm not good at following directions, and I can get lost or turned around in just about any location. As a result, many times I have thought, "How did I get here?"

For example, Donna and I planned our vacation to Hawaii for months. We read brochures, travel ads, maps, and searched the internet to help us make a "must see and do" list. We finalized the schedule and knew exactly where we would be each day. Our hotel was on Lewers Street in Honolulu and convenient to all the surrounding areas. But as with most vacations, there always seems to be an unknown factor lurking out there. With this vacation, it was Donna getting sick.

It all started about a day before we were to leave. Her head was stuffy and she was not feeling great. She insisted her condition would get better in a day or so. Confident with her diagnosis, we headed out the next day. During the flight I could tell her condition was not improving. When we arrived at the hotel with our dear friends, Louia and Diane, they insisted on getting some rest after the flight. Actually, they wanted Donna to get some rest.

Now before I go any further, I have to enlighten you on the relationship of Donna to most medicines. The warning "This medicine may make you drowsy" was written specifically for her. She can touch a bottle of antihistamine tablets and go to sleep. Anyway, she did take some medicine and got a good night's rest.

The next day, we all wanted to see as much as we could. Donna continued to doctor herself with over the counter medicine. Meanwhile, knowing she may not remember where she had been and what she had seen, I took a lot of photos so I could show her later. By evening, her condition had not improved. Instead, it had gotten worse. Being a long way from home and not knowing a good doctor, our best option was to call our family doctor, Dr. Morris. He made the diagnosis and a prescription was called in to a local pharmacy. With Louia driving, we got the medicine and were soon back at the hotel. I gave Donna the first round of medicine, and she was soon out for the night.

Since it was still early, I decided to go and purchase some souvenirs. I had seen several shops near the hotel, so I assumed the trip would only take about 30 to 45 minutes. I went directly to the shops and purchased a few items. Going back to the room, I saw some shops less than a block away and decided to check them out. I went in the front door facing the street but didn't see anything I wanted. I saw a side door leading to another shop and went inside. From there I went to another shop and finally to one last shop. Realizing I had to get back to the room, I went to what I thought was the street from where I had entered. Looking up, I saw street names that I didn't recognize. I knew I had to be just one block over, so I walked to the next block. Again I looked up and there was another street name that I didn't recognize. I looked up and down the street and didn't see anything familiar. I thought to myself, "How did I get here?" I didn't have my GPS (Donna) with me, and I knew I was in trouble.

Knowing I needed to get back to Donna, I had to do the unthinkable – ask for directions. I entered the lobby of a hotel to seek help. I went over and asked the doorman, "Sir, would you direct me to Lewers Street?" The reply was understanding and kind. Pointing, he said, "Go down this street. Take a left at the corner and the next street will be Lewers Street." I followed his simple directions and in minutes was back in our room. To this very day I don't know how I got so turned around. My physical steps had carried me to a place where I had to say, "How did I get here?"

Jesus

My physical steps have not been the only steps to cause me to ask, "How did I get here?" I can remember when my spiritual steps resulted in the same question. But I am not alone. Some of the major characters in the Bible had reasons to think this.

In the book of Exodus, we find Moses in what seems to be a disastrous situation. Pharaoh's army is about to attack. Moses is enclosed by mountains and the Red Sea. The children of Israel are complaining saying, "It is all Moses' fault." Certainly Moses could have thought, "How did I get here?"

29

Another example is Joseph. As a youth his brothers hated him. They put him into a pit and later sold him as a slave. As a slave he was falsely accused by his master's wife of trying to rape her and was thrown into prison. In prison Joseph befriended the chief butler of the king and interpreted his dream. The dream told of the chief butler being placed back into the service of the king. The butler promised to remember Joseph when his dream came true. Instead, he forgot about Joseph for two years. Only when the king had a dream that no one could interpret did the chief butler remember Joseph. In Genesis 37:2, Joseph was 17 years old when he was sold into slavery. In Genesis 41:46, Joseph was 30 years old when Pharaoh made him second in command over Egypt. Therefore, he must have spent about 13 years of his life either as a slave or in prison and none of those years were due to actions of which he was guilty. No doubt, Joseph was a man who definitely could have asked, "How did I get here?"

In Matthew 9:9, Jesus tells a hated tax collector named Matthew to "follow me." Jesus was not speaking of His physical footsteps but to follow Him spiritually. During His three years with the disciples, Jesus told them what to expect as a result of following Him. Matthew, in chapter 10 of the Gospel that bears his name, writes just a sample of what they were told to expect. Later in chapter 26, Jesus tells the disciples that one of them would betray Him; Judas then leaves to betray Him. In Matthew 26:33-35, the remaining eleven disciples, including Matthew, were adamant they would never deny Christ.

> Peter answered and said to Him, "Even if all are made to stumble because of You, I will never be made to stumble." Jesus said to him, "Assuredly, I say to you that this night, before the rooster crows, you will deny Me three

times." Peter said to Him, "Even if I have to die with You, I will not deny You!" And so said all the disciples (Matthew 26:33-35).

Usually Peter is identified with saying, "Even if I have to die with You, I will not deny You!" Notice that he was not the only disciple to say that. All the disciples said this. "All" included Matthew. However, when Jesus was betrayed and arrested in Gethsemane, "they all forsook Him and fled" (Matthew 26:56b). Again, Matthew was part of that "all." Matthew fled. He ran. As he ran, he was probably not concerned about what was going to happen to Jesus or what was going to happen to his fellow disciples. He was concerned about Matthew. And by his very actions he was saying, "Legs, get me out of here," and was probably thinking "How did I get here?"

The apostle Paul could have thought the same thing. He was born a Roman citizen. He was taught by the famous rabbi, Gamaliel. He was well trained in Jewish traditions and in the Scriptures. He became a Jewish religious leader, a Pharisee. He was passionate in his beliefs that Christians were wrong and that Christianity should be wiped out.

> All this time Saul [Paul] was breathing down the necks of the Master's disciples, out for the kill. He went to the Chief Priest and got arrest warrants to take to the meeting places in Damascus so that if he found anyone there belonging to the Way, whether men or women, he could arrest them and bring them to Jerusalem. (Acts 9:1-2 MSG).

Saul (Paul) had power, recognition, respect and fear from other people. He was in control. Then on his way to

31

persecuting Christians in Damascus, he was struck down with light and heard the Lord instruct him in what to do. Paul's story continues:

> As he neared Damascus on his journey, suddenly a light from heaven flashed around him. He fell to the ground and heard a voice say to him, "Saul, Saul, why do you persecute me?" "Who are you, Lord?" Saul asked. "I am Jesus, whom you are persecuting," he replied. "Now get up and go into the city, and you will be told what you must do." The men traveling with Saul stood there speechless; they heard the sound but did not see anyone. Saul got up from the ground, but when he opened his eyes he could see nothing. So they led him by the hand into Damascus. For three days he was blind, and did not eat or drink anything (Acts 9:3-9 NIV).

I am confident that during this time Paul could have thought, "How did I get here?" However, the "how did I get here" situations had just started for Paul and for others linked to him.

> There was a disciple in Damascus by the name of Ananias. The Master spoke to him in a vision: "Ananias." "Yes Master," he answered. "Get up and go over to Straight Avenue. Ask at the house of Judas for a man from Tarsus. His name is Saul. He's there praying. He has just had a dream in which he saw a man named Ananias enter the house and lay hands on him so he could see again." Ananias protested,

"Master, you can't be serious. Everybody's talking about this man and the terrible things he's been doing, his reign of terror against your people in Jerusalem! And now he's shown up here with papers from the Chief Priest that give him license to do the same to us." But the Master said, "Don't argue. Go! I have picked him as my personal representative to non-Jews and kings and Jews. And now I'm about to show him what he's in for – the hard suffering that goes with this job" (Acts 9:10-16 MSG).

As Scripture points out, Ananias was a person the Lord used in the conversion of Saul (Paul). Knowing what Saul had done to try to destroy Christianity, Ananias was instructed to go minister to Saul. He didn't want to go. Ananias' words reveal to us what was on his mind. "Now he's [Saul] shown up here with papers from the Chief Priest that give him license to do the same to us" (Acts 9:14 MSG). Ananias was saying, "I don't trust Saul. It could be a trap. I don't want to go there." Maybe Ananias could already visualize himself standing at Saul's door knocking, knowing swords were on the other side and asking, "How did I get here?"

But it wasn't a trap. Paul, the great and powerful, surrendered to the call of the Lord and became a believer. But his life after becoming a Christian was not an easy life. In II Corinthians 11:23-29, Paul tells about being jailed more often, beaten up more times than I can count, and at death's door time after time.

I've been flogged five times with the Jews' thirty-nine lashes, beaten by Roman rods three times, pummeled with rocks once. I've been shipwrecked three times, and immersed in the open sea for a night and a day. In hard traveling year in and year out, I've had to ford rivers, fend off robbers, struggle with friends, struggle with foes. I've been at risk in the city, at risk in the country, endangered by desert sun and sea storm, and betrayed by those I thought were my brothers. I've known drudgery and hard labor, many a long and lonely night without sleep, many a missed meal, blasted by the cold, naked to the weather. And that's not the half of it, when you throw in the daily pressures and anxieties of all the churches (II Corinthians 11:23-28 MSG).

With all this happening to Paul, surely he thought, "How did I get here?"

At some point in our Christian life, I believe most have thought "How did I get here?" I am not talking about physically getting lost in an unfamiliar city and getting directions back to the hotel, but spiritually getting "lost." Not concerning salvation, but as a Christian finding ourselves in a situation or set of circumstances that causes us to say this.

I don't know if Moses, Joseph, Peter, Matthew, Paul or Ananias, said, "How did I get here?" Scripture doesn't give us that answer. With each person, I used the word "could." I certainly believe they could have. Whether they did or did not really doesn't matter. What *does* matter is the way they responded to their situation.

From a "human" point of view, all of them came to a point in their lives where they could have quit, but they didn't. With the Egyptian army about to attack, Moses could have just surrendered to the cries of the people. While in prison, Joseph could have thrown up his hands and given up. Peter and Matthew could have recanted and surrendered to the Roman officials. Paul and Ananias could have thought obedience was too dangerous and taken the safe way out and quit, but none of them gave up. They didn't know how their situations were going to end, but they did not quit.

Not only did they not quit, they were obedient.

> And the LORD said to Moses, "Why do you cry to Me? Tell the children of Israel to go forward. But lift up your rod, and stretch out your hand over the sea and divide it. And the children of Israel shall go on dry ground through the midst of the sea (Exodus 14:15-16).

> Then Moses stretched out his hand over the sea; and the LORD caused the sea to go back by a strong east wind all that night, and made the sea into dry land, and the waters were divided. So the children of Israel went into the midst of the sea on the dry ground, and the waters were a wall to them on their right hand and on their left (Exodus 14:21-22).

> But the Lord said to Ananias, "Go!" (Acts 9:15a NIV).

> And Ananias went (Acts 9:17a).

> [Paul] He trembling and astonished said, "Lord, what wilt thou have me to do?" And the Lord said unto him, "Arise, and go into the city, and it shall be told thee what thou must do" (Acts 9:6 KJV).

> "Then Saul (Paul) arose" (Acts 9:8).

They did not quit. They were obedient. And they recognized that God was in control. For example, Joseph did not pity himself nor did he take revenge on his brothers. Instead, Joseph saw his hardships and adversities as a sovereign act of God.

> And God sent me [Joseph] before you to preserve a posterity for you in the earth, and to save your lives by a great deliverance. So now *it was* not you *who* sent me here, but God (Genesis 45:7-8a).

They did not quit. They were obedient. They recognized who was in control. And they knew that it was not about them but about God. God was to receive the glory. God makes it very clear with Moses, Joseph, Peter, Matthew, Paul and Ananias who was to receive the glory.

God said to Moses, "I [God] will gain glory" (Exodus 14:17b NIV). "The LORD was with Joseph" (Genesis 39:2a) and again "the LORD was with Joseph" (Genesis 39:21a). Peter wrote, "to Him be glory and dominion forever and ever. Amen" (I Peter 5:11). Paul wrote, "Therefore, whether you eat or drink, or whatever you do, do all to the glory of God" (I Corinthians 10:31).

In all these situations or circumstances they could have said, "How did I get here?" Instead, they did not quit, were obedient, recognized who was in control, and gave glory to God. Even during my "How did I get here?" moment on vacation, I did not quit. If I had, I would still be on a corner of some street begging for bread. I was obedient to the doorman's instructions. I recognized God was in control. He had promised never to forsake me, and I certainly gave Him glory when I got back to my hotel.

You

Just like me getting lost, a lot of difficult situations and circumstances are our own fault. Like the following illustration by Donald Grey Barnhouse, we let things get out of our reach.

> A small boy sailed his toy boat on a pond. The boat floated out of his reach, and he appealed to a larger boy to help him. This boy, without saying a word, picked up rocks and began throwing them out near the boat. The small boy pleaded with him not to hit his boat, but the big boy kept on. Soon the small boy noticed that each stone was falling on the far side of the boat, making a wave that pushed it nearer the shore. Then he realized that the big boy was planning the fall of each stone in order to bring the boat nearer to the shore. Soon it was within reach and the owner had his boat again.
>
> We must never forget that God plans the fall of each stone within our circumstances, and that each storm and wave is calculated by Him in order to bring us nearer to Himself.[2]

Even when we cause our own sorrow and trouble, we can call upon our Lord for help. We can ask Him to forgive us and to take control of our lives.

However, there are times when God has allowed us to be placed in a difficult situation, and it seems to be no fault of our own. It is especially in those times we may think, "How did I get here?" A. W. Tozer had wonderful insight into those difficult situations. He wrote,

> To the child of God, there is no such thing as an accident. He travels an appointed way...

Accidents may indeed appear to befall him and misfortune stalk his way; but these evils will be so in appearance only and will seem evil only because we cannot read the secret script of God's hidden providence and so cannot discover the ends at which He aims...The man of true faith may live in the absolute assurance that his steps are ordered by the Lord."[3]

Psalm 37:23 tells us that "the steps of a good man are ordered by the Lord." Not like my steps to Lewers Street but steps of life from one area/place to another. The steps that Moses, Paul and Joseph took were ordered and guided by God. May you accept Him as your Lord and follow Him. Don't quit. Be obedient. Recognize who is in control and give all the glory to God. Then when you think, "How did I get here," you will know how. Your steps were ordered by the Lord.

Chapter 4: Combo #2, Jesus and You

"Today's decisions are tomorrow's realities."[1]

Combo # 2

As a businessman I would often visit various customers throughout my area. Sometimes I would devote most of the day to one customer, including lunch. On other trips, I would try to arrange to see as many people as possible. In order to accomplish that goal, I would use the drive-thru at a "burger doodle" to save time. This may sound strange, but many times I would go through the drive-thru, order my lunch, and then park in their parking lot. I would eat my lunch and prepare for the afternoon meetings. If I were behind in my schedule, I would use the drive-thru and eat as I traveled. I admit that eating fast food is not a healthy decision and eating while driving is not safe. I certainly would rather sit down at a good "meat and three," but I had to choose between staying on schedule or not.

Life requires decisions. Some are good and some are bad. Some are life changing and some are insignificant. The simple act of getting lunch sounds simple, but it required hundreds of decisions. I had to decide what I wanted to eat. Do I want a hamburger, a chicken sandwich, a roast beef sandwich or something else? Should I drive further to get what I want or go to the most convenient place? With a double drive through, do I go left or right? This requires all kinds of decisions - turn the steering wheel, lower the window, slow down, stop, look at the menu. Should I have Combo #1, Combo #2, or some other choice? Do I want to "supersize" it or not?

Still, more decisions will be required before I can eat. I have to decide whether I will have fries, onion rings, a baked potato, or carrot/raisin salad? Will I have a soft drink, sweet tea, a shake, coffee, or water? Finally, I decide what I am going to order. I have to talk to a machine. Do I talk loudly or softly? Do I try to find the correct change? Do I even have correct change? After paying, I reach for my sack of food only to be asked to make more decisions. "Do you need any mayo, ketchup, or salt with your order?" Decisions, decisions, decisions. It makes my head spin just to think of all the decisions I had to make just to get a chicken sandwich, carrot salad, and sweet tea.

When you look at life, you see that life is a series of decisions. Each day starts with decisions. Are you going to open your eyes or not? Are you going to get out of bed? Are you going to put your right foot or your left foot on the floor first? Are you going to scratch you head? Are you going to get a shower? Are you going to eat breakfast? Are you going to brush your teeth? Are you going to go to work? What are you going to wear? Are you going to have some quiet time in the morning? The list of morning decisions could go on and on.

Decisions continue all throughout the day. It makes no difference whether you work at a business or at home, you still have to make decisions. Do you go the speed limit or not? Do you buy gasoline or wait until the afternoon? Do you rub your burning eyes? Do you speak to a stranger? Do you pick up milk and bread before you go home? Even at the end of the day, you are still making decisions. What TV program are you going to watch? Do you go to bed before or after the news? Do you sleep with or without a blanket? Do you set the alarm? Do you pray before going to bed? Do you sleep on your right side, your left side, your back or stomach? Decisions, decisions, decisions. You cannot *not* make decisions! Even if you say, "I am not going to make any decisions today," you made a decision. I tried to find some scientific statistic to quote as to the number of decisions a person makes in one day, but I couldn't find one. Anyway, how could anyone calculate the number of decisions a person makes in one day? It would be impossible.

Jesus

Decisions have always been a fact of life. Even before Adam and Eve made the decision to eat from the tree of knowledge, Adam had decided the "names to all cattle, to the birds of the air, and to every beast of the field" (Genesis 2:20). All throughout the Bible, we see good and bad decisions being made. In Genesis chapter 6, Noah had to decide whether or not to build an ark. In Genesis 12, Abraham had to decide whether or not to leave his homeland. In I Samuel 13, Saul had to decide whether or not to wait on Samuel. In II Samuel 11, David had to decide whether or not to commit or not to commit adultery with Bathsheba. In Ruth 1, Ruth had to decide to stay with her people or go with Naomi. In Exodus 3, Moses had to decide whether or not to lead the children of Israel out of Egypt.

After Moses died, Joshua had to decide to accept or reject the responsibility of becoming the new leader of the children of Israel. This was not an insignificant decision. As a leader,

Joshua had no MBA or any other college degree. He had no laptop, no Internet, and no GPS. But he did have a promise from the Lord. "As I was with Moses, so I will be with you; I will never leave you nor forsake you" (Joshua 1:5b NIV). Then the Lord encourages and instructs Joshua.

> Be strong and of good courage, for to this people you shall divide as an inheritance the land which I swore to their fathers to give them. Only be strong and very courageous, that you may observe to do according to all the law which Moses My servant commanded you; do not turn from it to the right hand or to the left, that you may prosper wherever you go (Joshua 1:6-7).

Joshua had to decide to believe God or not. This is more than Combo #1 or Combo #2. One can only imagine all the thoughts that must have gone through Joshua's mind. Whatever Joshua was thinking, God answered his thoughts by asking a rhetorical question. "Have I not commanded you? Be strong and of good courage; do not be afraid, nor be dismayed, for the Lord your God is with you wherever you go" (Joshua 1:9). Based on what God said, we see Joshua's decision in verse 10. He takes command. He believes and obeys God. As a result, Joshua saw the water of the Jordan River stand still and rise up in a heap (Joshua 3:16). He saw the walls of Jericho fall (Joshua 6:20). He saw the Lord slay more of the enemy with hailstones than the children of Israel did with the sword (Joshua 10:11). He saw the sun and the moon stand still (Joshua 10:13) and he saw God send hornets to defeat an army (Joshua 24:12). He saw all of this because of a decision to believe/trust God.

In the New Testament, Jesus was continually asking

people to make decisions. In His early ministry, a simple statement like "Follow me" required a decision. In the ninth chapter of the Gospel of Matthew, Jesus called Matthew to come and follow Him. Matthew was a tax collector, which was a very lucrative position but was hated by everyone, especially the Jews. Nevertheless, Matthew made the decision to follow Jesus.

In the Gospel of Matthew, we find a rich young man who decides not to follow Jesus. Jesus said to him, "Go sell your possessions; give everything to the poor. All your wealth will then be in heaven. Then come follow me" (Matthew 19:21 MSG). Unlike Matthew, the rich young man decided not to follow Jesus and as a result the young man "went away sorrowful, for he had great possessions" (Matthew 19:22b). Remember, Matthew was an eye witness to this incident. We can only wonder what may have been going through Matthew's mind when he wrote this. He could relate to a person that had possessions. Matthew had heard the same words, "Follow me." But Matthew did give it all up and followed Jesus. Now he was watching a young man make the most horrible decision that was possible. I am sure Matthew's heart went out to the young man, but Matthew could not force him to make the decision he himself had made. Both had to make their own decision.

One question that Jesus asked Peter continues to be one that is asked of all of us and it demands a decision. The question that Jesus asked was, "Who do you say that I am?" Peter answered and said, "You are the Christ, the Son of the living God" (Matthew 16:16). Jesus was asked a similar question when He was on trial before the Sanhedrin.

> Again the high priest asked Him, saying to Him, "Are You the Christ, the Son of the Blessed?" Jesus said, "I am. And you will see

the Son of Man sitting at the right hand of the Power, and coming with the clouds of heaven." Then the high priest tore his clothes and said, "What further need do we have of witnesses? You have heard the blasphemy! What do you think?" And they all condemned Him to be deserving of death (Mark 14:61b-64).

All of these people had to make a decision as to who Jesus was. Matthew, the disciples, and Peter made the right decision. The rich man and the High Priest made the wrong decision. This question continues to be asked of all of us today. Who do *you* say Jesus is? Is He the greatest liar that has ever lived? Is He the Son of God? Is He the Messiah? Is He God? It may not be verbal, but deep down in the very soul of each person, the question is being asked and it demands a decision. While on earth, Matthew, the rich man, Peter and the High Priest all stood close to Jesus physically, but each made a decision that affected their eternal relationship with Jesus – eternal separation or eternal fellowship. Leading theologian and author Herschel H. Hobbs wrote:

> Someone said there is a point in the Rocky Mountains where raindrops fall ever so close together. However, those falling on one side of the ridge flow westward toward the Pacific Ocean; those falling on the other side of the ridge flow southeastward toward the Gulf of Mexico. The raindrops fall so near each other, but wind up so far apart.
>
> This may be an apt illustration of people making decisions for Christ. Persons may be in the same family or social group. Yet their decisions for or against Christ determine

whether their eternal destiny is heaven or hell. At the moment the difference may seem so slight. But destinies are bound up in the decisions they make. Persons are to ponder long in deciding about so vital a matter.[2]

You

The more we study the Bible, the more we come to the conclusion that the Bible is a book of decisions for individuals in the past, present and future. Life requires decisions every minute of every day. Look left or right. Be silent or say something. Sit or stand. Go or stay. Eat or fast. Work or play. Even as you read this, you have to decide to read more or stop here.

Yet, there are some matters we didn't have to decide. For example, we didn't decide when we were born. We didn't decide who our parents would be. We didn't decide the color of our hair or the shape of our nose. We didn't decide the place of our birth or where we would live as a child. We didn't decide what baby clothes to wear or what toys to buy. We didn't decide where to go to school. Nevertheless, God has allowed us to make the most important decision that an individual will ever make. No one else can decide where you will spend eternity. Only you can make that decision.

If you choose Combo #2 and it really doesn't taste as you had expected, the consequences of that decision will be a disappointing meal, but it will not matter in a day or so. If you choose a used car that looks great, but after 500 miles it becomes a lemon, more financial expenses will be the consequences, but it really won't matter in a hundred years.

But the decision to believe who Jesus is has eternal consequences. That decision *will* matter in a hundred years, a thousand years, a million years, a trillion years, forever and forever. Jesus said, "Most assuredly, I say to you, he who hears My word and believes in Him who sent Me has everlasting life, and shall not come into judgment, but has passed from death into life" (John 5:24). Not only do we have everlasting life, "we are heirs – heirs of God and co-heirs with Christ, if indeed we share in his sufferings in order that we may also share in his glory" (Romans 8:17 NIV).

> A king once said to a particular favorite, "Ask what thou wilt, and I will give it unto thee!" He [the favorite] thought, "If I ask to be made a general, I shall readily obtain it; if for half the kingdom, he will give it to me. I will ask for something to which all these things shall be added." So he said to the king, "Give me thy daughter to [be my] wife." This made him heir to all the wealth and honors of the kingdom. So choosing Christ makes us heirs to all the wealth and glory of the Father's kingdom.[3]

You didn't have a choice in the color of your eyes. You may have one blue eye and one brown eye. You didn't have a choice of who would be your parents. You may have the worst parents in the world. They may have abused you in every way. You didn't have a choice where you lived as a child. The list of "You didn't have a choice in" could go on and on. But you and you alone will make the most important decision in your life. You must decide to trust Jesus or not. Where you spend eternity is your choice.

Chapter 5: Computers, Jesus and You

> *"People change, fashions change,*
> *and conditions change,*
> *but God never changes"[1]*

Computers

As a baby boomer, I have seen change in a lot of areas. For example, portable phones were a rarity, and certainly not for the common person. If you did see one, it was held in a pouch, not in your hand. Some of us had "party lines." You actually shared a phone line with other households. I think our party line had about four families on it. Usually, when you lifted the receiver to make a call, you could hear someone else talking. When you were able to talk, you never knew how many other folks were listening in.

On a trip you would look at a map not a GPS. In our rural area, you were fortunate to be able to receive three TV stations. AM radio was dominant. Most of the high school students didn't drive themselves to school. If a person did drive, they could go to a full service gas station where the attendant would pump the gas, clean the windshield and check the oil. For a younger generation reading this, believe it or not you didn't have to get out of your car. But you paid in cash not with a credit card. If you didn't have the cash, you didn't buy the gas. I could go on but you get the picture. Boomers have seen a lot of change, but the generation before us, the great generation, has seen many more changes. Television, space exploration, nuclear power plants, atomic bombs, mobile phones, microwave ovens, and advances in medicine are just a few of the technologies that have come into being during their generation.

One thing that has had a tremendous influence on both generations is the computer. Throughout the world, you can find computers in billions of homes. Computers are not only in homes. You can see laptops, iPads, smartphones, etc. in libraries, schools, churches, and just about anywhere you go. Computers have become common fixtures in everyday life.

Not only has the computer changed our way of life, it has added meanings to some words. The word *boot* means something more than footwear. The word *clipboard* is not necessarily a hard board with a metal clip at the top. A *mouse* can have a wire instead of a tail. A *virus* is not just a physical sickness. *Paste* is more than glue. The list can go on and on, but you see what I mean. Definitely, the following list would not be such a joke in the 1950s:

THE VERMONTER'S GUIDE TO COMPUTER LINGO
Modem:	What you did to the hayfields.
Windows:	What to shut when it's 30 below.
Log On:	Making the wood stove hotter.
Hard Drive:	Getting home during mud season.
Microchips:	What are left in the bag when the big chips are gone.
Download:	Getting the firewood off the pickup.
Megahertz:	What you get when you're not careful downloading.[2]

Computers affect our economy. They generate jobs and create income not only in the production of the unit but in other ways. For instance, when I purchase a computer, it is a necessity for me to purchase a support agreement. However, support is just a drop in the bucket when compared to the millions of jobs and the amount of income created by the worldwide commerce made possible by the computer.

I must admit that I know very little about my computer. I am learning. I know enough to email, use the Internet for news, weather, financial items, and to "Google" information. I have also come to appreciate my computer more and more, especially when preparing a sermon. The computer has so many more features than the typewriter. It will capitalize some of the words that I fail to capitalize and makes me aware of errors in grammar and spelling. It will allow me to move paragraphs around, change the size of the text, and much more.

One thing that is very evident is that computers do exactly what you tell them to do, and I do tell my computer a lot of erroneous things to do. In other words, I make a lot of errors. As a result, my favorite feature of my computer is the undo arrow. This little arrow is a blessing to all of us who make errors. It will actually allow me to undo the errors I have made. I simply acknowledge the error, go to the undo arrow, click the mouse, and the error is gone. Then I simply replace the error with the correct entry.

In life there are countless stories of individuals who would have liked to undo some of the errors they had made. For example, I am sure Gary Kildall could have used an undo arrow.

In 1973 Gary Kildall wrote the first popular operating system for personal computers, named CP/M. According to writer Phillip Fiorini, IBM approached Kildall in 1980 about

49

Odenville Public Library
P O Box 249
Odenville, AL 35120

developing the operating system for IBM PCs. But Kildall snubbed IBM officials at a crucial meeting, according to another author, Paul Carroll. The day IBM came calling he chose to fly his new airplane. The frustrated IBM executives turned instead to Bill Gates, founder of a small software company called Microsoft, and his operating system named MS-DOS.[3]

Making or losing billions of dollars is trivial compared to the possibilities an undo arrow could do for individuals. For example, if we had an undo arrow, mothers could undo the loss of their sons or daughters in war. Godly leaders could undo the suffering caused by the previous uncaring dictatorial leaders. Families could undo the words that have kept family members from speaking to each other for years. Churches could undo quarrels that have divided and damaged the cause of Christ.

The undo arrow for individuals sounds like a great idea. Actually, even if there were such an arrow, it would not solve any of the problems. As a matter of fact, we would still have the same problems that we have today and that have existed for thousands of years. The reason I say this is simple. For example, a mother may undo the cause of war. At the same time, a mad dictator would be using his undo arrow to change a lost battle into victory. So the conflict would continue. The family members that are not speaking would only undo the words of the other side of the family. A church member would use the undo arrow to change the suggestions of another church member. So the undo arrow would undo the "undo" that someone else had undone and the problems would still exist.

All of us have or have had situations, words, or actions in our lives that we would love to undo. No matter how much we would like to undo an action or take back words said in anger, it is impossible to do. However, when it comes to our relationship to God we do have an undo arrow and each individual has been given the opportunity to use it. It's a matter of choice and the wonderful thing about our very own personal spiritual undo arrow is that no one else can undo what you have undone. Let me explain.

Jesus

Man was created to have fellowship with God, but man sinned. "All have sinned" (Romans 3:23a).

> Sin is succinctly, inherently, and primarily anti-Godness. Sin is against God...Before it is anything else, sin is ungodliness.[4]

Also, "all unrighteousness is sin" (I John 5:17). Therefore, if all have sinned and sin is ungodliness and unrighteousness, then according to Romans 1:18a, "the wrath of God is revealed from heaven against all ungodliness and unrighteousness of men." Or, more simply, "He who believes in the Son has everlasting life; and he who does not believe the Son shall not see life, but the wrath of God abides on him" (John 3:36). In other words, "The wounding of his gracious love and rejection of his mercy evokes his holy wrath."[5]

The verses above, without a doubt, establish the fact that everyone has sinned. As a result of sin, the wrath of God abides (remains) on the individual. The word "wrath" can be connected with many words, such as "wrath of a nation" or "wrath of a storm" but all the words you could add to "wrath" could never begin to approach the magnitude of the "wrath of God." Anyone with any intelligence should never want to experience the wrath of God. Yet, we all have sinned, and as sinners we are under the wrath of God. This is definitely a situation where an undo arrow is needed. But how is this possible?

> Through his atoning sacrifice on Calvary, Christ set humankind free by taking the retribution of sin upon himself. He suffered the agony and shame that we deserve to suffer because of our sin. He thereby satisfied the just requirements of the law of God and at the same time turned away the wrath of God from fallen human kind.[6]

As we continue, we discover our need is not an undo arrow, but an undo person, and that person is Jesus. "Since we have now been justified by his blood, how much more shall we be saved from God's wrath through him!" (Romans 5:9 NIV). And as believers, we now "wait for his Son from heaven, whom he raised from the dead —Jesus, who rescues us from the coming wrath" (I Thessalonians 1:10 NIV).

As you can see, the only way to undo the broken fellowship is through Jesus Christ. Fellowship cannot be restored in religion or attending church or in sacraments or ordinances. However, just to know that sin is the "error" and to know Jesus is the only way to "undo" the error is not enough. In order for the undo Person to undo the broken relationship, action must be taken. For example, the computer may show you the spelling error, but you have to act upon that notice. The same is true with our relationship with God. Romans 6:23 tells us, "The wages of sin is death, but the gift of God is eternal life through Jesus Christ our Lord." Just like any other gift, we have to decide to accept or reject the gift. Some people make receiving the gift too hard. They think there are strings attached like the announcement you receive in the mail about a great "gift" for you. All you have to do is buy a magazine. But with "the gift of God" everything has been paid for by Jesus. To receive "the gift of God" we must believe: "That if you will confess with your mouth the Lord Jesus and believe in your heart that God has raised Him from the dead you shall be saved" (Romans 10:9). For the person that has never come to Jesus and asked for forgiveness, these verses promise to undo a relationship with God from an adversarial relationship to a loving relationship with God. After receiving the gift, you will have a personal relationship with God. His Spirit will come and live within you. For the person that has a personal relationship with God, which has been broken by sin, the undo Person will bring forgiveness and restore the relationship with God. "If we confess our sins, He is faithful and just to forgive us *our* sins, and to cleanse us from all unrighteousness" (I John 1:9).

You

We are promised that God wants to forgive us. "For You, Lord, are good, and ready to forgive, and abundant in mercy to all those who call upon You" (Psalm 86:5). One of the last statements Jesus made was to ask forgiveness for the ones that were crucifying Him. "Father, forgive them, for they do not know what they do" (Luke 23:34). So it is not a matter of you having an undo Person or not. It is a matter of using the undo Person that God has provided. If you have led a perfect life, then you don't need an undo Person. For the rest of us, we realize the necessary need for an undo Person in our life and we thank God for providing and promising that He will forgive us. Then we can continue our life knowing our sins have been forgiven and fellowship has been restored.

In either situation, as with the computer, the course of action is the same. First, we have to realize we have a problem. In our relationship with God, we have to admit that sin is the problem. We have to want to do what it takes to undo the error/sin. Then we act in faith upon that decision. That action results in sin being undone/forgiven, but we don't stop there. We must take action to replace the error. In the case of typing, we type the correct words. Spiritually, we repent and the Holy Spirit replaces self as the boss of our life. We must remember that the consequences of either sin or an error typing take time and effort to correct.

Once I heard an excellent explanation of sin and God's plan to defeat sin in our lives. I have it written in the front of my Bible. I cannot remember who it was that said it, but it has meant a lot to me over the years. He simply said:

> Salvation is a onetime event. As a result, we have been saved from the penalty of sin. We have been made righteous. This is known as justification.
>
> As we continue to live our lives and grow as a Christian, we yield more and more control to the Holy Spirit who lives within. This is a process. As a result, we are being saved from the power of sin. This is known as sanctification.
>
> Then one day, we will say it is finished and go on to be with the Lord. As a result, we will be saved from the very presence of sin. This is known as glorification.

The undo arrow is a wonderful function and is valuable while using the computer. But when life is over, it really won't be important if you used the undo arrow or not. However, when this life is over, it really *will* matter if you used the undo Person/Jesus Christ or not.

Chapter 6: Elvis, Jesus and You

"The good life exists only when we stop wanting a better one. The itch for things is a virus draining the soul of contentment."[1]

Elvis

When I say the word "Elvis," what do you think of? Of course, the answer will vary depending on the person. One person may think of "The King of Rock and Roll." Another person may think of Graceland or the Ed Sullivan Show where many thought Elvis was too offensive with his "shake, rattle and roll." The list of things that people may say would be overwhelming. Being an Elvis Presley fan, there would be a long list of things that I would think of. I would think of the Elvis concert that Donna and I attended in 1976. At the concert, we saw a packed house of screaming fans and ladies fighting for a scarf Elvis had used to wipe sweat from his brow, a typical show that only Elvis could do. Of course, at the end of the concert, we would hear those famous words: "Elvis has left the building." Also, when I think of Elvis, I think of a person who served his country in the Army. I think of a person who could sing some songs like no one else could,

55

songs like "Memories," "American Trilogy," "Welcome To My World," "Suspicious Minds," "I'll Remember You" and "Can't Help Falling In Love." Or, I may think of some movies Elvis starred in such as *Love Me Tender, Blue Hawaii, Follow That Dream,* or *Paradise Hawaiian Style.* Low budget movies with very little plot, pretty girls and Elvis as the hero were popular and profitable. Elvis appeared to be a person who had everything going for him. Yet, there seemed to be something missing or something wrong – a life that gave the impression of no contentment and a never ending search for happiness. "Just before his death at age forty-two, he wished he could find one week when he could just live a normal life, going up and down the streets of his city without being harassed. He would pay a million dollars, for one week of peace."[2]

There was another singer before Elvis that seemed to be on top of the world, attracting screaming crowds. They wanted the clothes off his back. This person was in a "rocking jailhouse" hundreds of years before Elvis was in *Jailhouse Rock.* But his life was different in many ways. The singer's name was Paul. We have no CDs, LPs, cassettes, movies or DVDs of Paul. However, we have Paul's story told in the greatest of all books, the Bible. In chapter 16 of Acts, we find Paul on a missionary trip. During this trip, Paul met a young slave girl who was possessed by "a spirit of divination." She "brought her masters much gain by soothsaying." "In the name of Jesus Christ," Paul commanded the spirit to come out of her and it did. Realizing their money making slave girl could no longer make money for them, they dragged Paul and his companion Silas into the marketplace before the authorities, charging them with "customs unlawful for us Romans to accept or practice." The crowds came and joined in the attack. Paul and Silas were stripped, beaten, and placed in jail with their feet bound.

But at midnight Paul and Silas were praying and singing hymns to God, and the prisoners were listening to them. Suddenly there was a great earthquake, so that the foundations of the prison were shaken; and immediately all the doors were opened and everyone's chains were loosed. And the keeper of the prison, awaking from sleep and seeing the prison doors open, supposing the prisoners had fled, drew his sword and was about to kill himself (Acts 16: 25-27).

The jailer was responsible for the prisoners and would be punished if they escaped, probably with the death sentence. Before the jailer killed himself, Paul shouts out, "Don't kill yourself. We are still here. We have not left the building." (my paraphrase of Acts 16:28).

Then he [the jailer] called for a light, ran in, and fell down trembling before Paul and Silas. And he brought them out and said, "Sirs, what must I do to be saved?" So they said, "Believe on the Lord Jesus Christ, and you will be saved, you and your household." Then they spoke the word of the Lord to him and to all who were in his house. And he took them the same hour of the night and washed their stripes. And immediately he and all his family were baptized. Now when he had brought them into his house, he set food before them; and he rejoiced, having believed in God with all his household (Acts 16:29-34).

What a difference between Elvis and Paul. From a human standpoint, one seemed to be on top of the world with no joy in his life, and the other rejoicing in the very pit of the earth. One was singing to an audience of thousands and the other was singing to an audience of One. One couldn't find satisfaction or contentment in life, and the other found contentment in whatever situation he was in. As a matter of fact, in a letter to the Philippians Paul wrote:

> I have learned to be content in whatever circumstances I am. I know both how to have a little, and I know how to have a lot. In any and all circumstances I have learned the secret of being content – whether well-fed or hungry, whether in abundance or in need. I am able to do all things through Him [Jesus Christ] who strengthens me (Philippians 4:11b-14 HCSB).

Paul realized that real contentment was a result of what was going on inside of a person - not what was happening on the outside. He realized and taught that if our contentment can be changed by what's going on outside of us, we can never be content because what's going on outside of us is always changing.

To better understand this statement, all we have to do is to look at the definition of contented. Webster's dictionary defines "contented" as being "satisfied or manifesting satisfaction with one's possessions, status, or situation."[3] Notice the word "satisfaction." Satisfaction with one's possessions, status, or situation is how to be content. Based on that definition, no one can always be content because these are outward things. Every day a person lives, his possessions grow older, social status changes with circumstances, and situations change like the weather. The following story reminds me that human nature cannot be satisfied or contented.

The story tells of a mother and son who lived in a forest. One day when they were out a tornado surprised them. The mother clung to a tree and tried to hold her son. But the swirling winds carried him into the sky. He was gone. The woman began to weep and pray: "Please, O Lord, bring back my boy! He's all I have. I'd do anything not to lose him. If you'll bring him back, I'll serve you all my days." Suddenly the boy toppled from the sky, right at her feet—a bit mussed up, but safe and sound. His mother joyfully brushed him off. Then she stopped for a moment, looked to the sky, and said, "He had a hat, Lord."[4]

We may laugh at the story, but it does bring home the truth of how contentment can change into discontentment. For example, Paul had possessions, status and his situation in life was exceptional. But Paul (then called Saul) was not satisfied with persecuting some Christians. He wanted all believers to be eradicated. He asked and received permission to go to Damascus "so that if he found any who were of the Way, whether men or women, he might bring them bound to Jerusalem" (Acts 9:2). If he had thrown 1,000 Christians in prison, he would not have been satisfied. He would have wanted 2,000 the next time. The persecution of Christians became Paul's own personal war. Today it is no different. If a person sells one million records one year, and sells 750,000 the next, that person is not content. Or if a salesman breaks past sales records, he will not be content unless he sells more the next year.

In the syndicated cartoon "Mister Boffo" Joe Martin pictures a middle-aged man lying on a psychologist's couch. The psychologist sits on a chair next to him, listens intently, and writes in a notebook. The man on the couch has a problem. "I drive a Mercedes," he says, "I have a beach house in Bermuda, a 12-room penthouse, a 90-foot yacht. My clothes are made by the finest tailors in London. I have a world-class wine cellar. And yet I'm still not happy." The psychologist asks, "Do you have a Rolex?" Abruptly the troubled man raises his head from the couch, points his finger in the air, and declares, "Why no, I don't!"

Such is the folly of those who pursue happiness in material possessions. They will always be one purchase away from a happy life.[5]

It is the same for any whose contentment is based on possessions, status or situation. The contentment begins to fade and becomes discontentment.

Jesus

The "Parable of the Rich Fool" is found in Luke 12. In this parable, Jesus teaches contentment is not found in being "satisfied or manifesting satisfaction with one's possessions, status or situation" as Webster's dictionary states. Instead of contentment, discontentment is the result of a person depending on possessions, status or a situation.

> And He [Jesus] said to them, "Take heed and beware of covetousness, for one's life does not consist in the abundance of the things he possesses." Then He spoke a parable to them,

saying: "The ground of a certain rich man yielded plentifully. And he thought within himself, saying, 'What shall I do, since I have no room to store my crops?' So he said, 'I will do this: I will pull down my barns and build greater, and there I will store all my crops and my goods. And I will say to my soul, "Soul, you have many goods laid up for many years; take your ease; eat, drink, *and* be merry." But God said to him, 'Fool! This night your soul will be required of you; then whose will those things be which you have provided?'" (Luke 12:15b-20).

Notice the rich fool had to build greater barns. He was not content with what he had. Evidently, he found no contentment or satisfaction with his possessions, status, or situation. He was discontent with the barns he had and believed building greater barns would make him content. The thrill of building would be satisfaction in itself, but he was wrong. Human nature cannot be satisfied or contented with possessions, status or situations. This was true in Jesus' day and is true today.

One strategy of Satan is to make a believer discontent. If the enemy can do this, he is well on his way of making the person ineffective. Experts in marketing know how powerful discontentment is. Make the person discontent with an existing product and soon a new product will take its place. The old car may be great transportation, but it just doesn't look good. The solution is to buy a new car. The problem seems to be solved, but in reality a bigger problem has been created. Debt will soon cause discontentment again. The new car payment may be manageable but tight. Then an emergency expense comes up and there is not enough money to cover the car payment *and* the conversation turns to "why did you have to buy that car?" The downward spiral intensifies at an increasing rate: Contentment to discontentment to destruction.

But Christians should be content. Paul said, "I have learned in whatever state I am, to be content" (Philippians 4:11). Paul *learned* to be content. He just didn't wake up one day and say, "I am content." He learned it. It was and is a process. It is the process of becoming more like Christ. Contentment is the result of a right relationship with God and recognizing that God is sovereign. Paul had all that Webster's Dictionary had used to define contentment: possessions, status, and an imposing situation. But God changed him from within. Paul could have continued to persecute Christians. He would have had his moment of glory in history. From a human point of view, his life would probably have been easier. Instead, he trusted Christ and had contentment based on what was going on inside of him, not what was going on outside of him. He was content writing letters to individuals and churches from prison as the Holy Spirit directed him. Little did Paul know these letters would be a large part of the New Testament, nor did he have any idea the impact those letters to individuals and churches would have on Christianity. Paul may not have known why God was allowing him to be in a prison, but there was one thing Paul did know. He knew the promise God had made through the prophet Isaiah. "Fear not, for I *am* with you; Be not dismayed, for I *am* your God. I will strengthen you, Yes, I will help you, I will uphold you with My righteous right hand" (Isaiah 41:10).

You

The question is not "Was Elvis content?" The question is not "Was Paul content?" The question is "Are you content?" Can you say with Paul, "I have learned, in whatsoever state I am, to be content." If you have never accepted Christ as you personal Savior, you will never be content. If you are a Christian that has substituted things for a relationship with the Lord, you will not be content. In either situation, you will always be searching but never finding. If you believe being "satisfied with one's possessions, status, or situation" will bring you contentment, you are believing a lie. This belief will result in discontentment instead of contentment. As a matter of fact, if contentment is based on possessions, status or situation, then a person will never be content. C. S. Lewis in *The Screwtape Letters* wrote: "And all the time the joke is that the word 'Mine' in its fully possessive sense cannot be uttered by human being about anything...They will find out in the end, never fear, to whom their time, their souls, and their bodies really belong – certainly not to *them*, whatever happens."[6] So, you can believe the Bible or the dictionary. Which will it be?

If you are worth a billion dollars, then a little more money is necessary. If you have a new car, it will get old and a new one will fill the gap, but only until it gets old. Whatever "it" is, it will not satisfy. Just like the thirst for water, your thirst for contentment will return again. You will need more of it to drink to satisfy your thirst.

> Don't be obsessed with getting more material things. Be relaxed with what you have. Since God assured us, "I'll never let you down, never walk off and leave you," we can boldly quote, "God is there, ready to help; I'm fearless no matter what. Who or what can get to me?" (Hebrews 13:5-6 MSG).
>
> Pat Boone said of Elvis, "I cared a lot for Elvis." He said, "He went in the wrong direction. Ironically, we met for the last time

when I was going toward the East and he was on his way to Las Vegas. He said to me, 'Say, Pat, where you going?' And I told him I was going to be involved in some kind of ministry. And he says, 'Hey, I'm going to Vegas. Pat, as long as I've known you, you've been going in the wrong direction.' Pat Boone answered, 'Elvis, that just depends on where you're coming from and where you're going.'"[7]

Where are you coming from and where are you going? I pray you are going to a place in your life where you find true contentment – not in your possessions, status, or situation, but in your relationship to Jesus Christ because all those external things will not last. As the apostle James wrote, "For what is your life? It is even a vapor that appears for a little time, and then vanishes away" (James 5:14b).

We who follow Christ are men and women of eternity. We must put no confidence in the passing scenes of the disappearing world. We must resist every attempt of Satan to palm off upon us the values that belong to mortality. Nothing less than forever is long enough for us. We view with amused sadness the frenetic scramble of the world to gain a brief moment in the sun.[8]

As people of eternity, only in eternal things will we find contentment. Everything else is just a vapor vanishing away. Only in Jesus Christ can a person find contentment.

Chapter 7: Mothers, Jesus and You

> *"Mothers write on the hearts of their children what the world's rough hand cannot erase."*[1]

Mothers

Mothers have been described by many writers. For example, John Killinger's book *Lost in Wonder, Love, and Praise* includes the following affirmation:

> I believe in the love of all mothers, and its importance in the lives of the children they bear. It is stronger than steel, softer than down, and more resilient than a green sapling on the hillside. It closes wounds, melts disappointments, and enables the weakest child to stand tall and straight in the fields of adversity.[2]

I certainly agree with what John Killinger wrote about mothers, but I have to add, all "mothers" are not mothers like I am talking about. Before I start writing about mothers, I want to make a couple of things very clear. First, just because a woman can give birth to a baby does not make that woman a mother like I'm talking about. Secondly, there are a lot of women that have never given birth to a child, but they are mothers. Let me give you a personal example of each.

My grandmother was born in Mississippi. Her father had a large farm and the family was not in need. When her father died, her mother was more concerned about her own welfare and having a good time. As a result, the farm was lost and the four children were placed in an orphanage. My grandmother, the oldest child, was about seven or eight years old at that time. She had two sisters and one brother, the youngest being about eighteen months old. During the next ten to eleven years, Grandma helped take care of the other siblings and was a mother to them at the orphanage. Being the oldest, my grandmother left the orphanage at eighteen and established her own home in Alabama. As the other children left the orphanage, they all followed her.

Now my great grandmother was not a "mother" to any of the children, especially the three youngest ones. My grandmother was the "mother" to the three children. She was a "mother" to her three siblings before she became a mother to her own biological children. My grandmother taught by example the importance of being a mother that loved, sacrificed and cared for her children. For that reason, I was blessed with a wonderful mother. Also, I could not ask for a better mother for our boys than Donna. These two mothers, my mom and my wife, have been the most influential people in my life. They have been more influential than any pastor, more than any teacher or professor, more than anyone – period. Surely, I have been blessed with wonderful mothers – my wife, my mom and my grandmother, but my great-grandmother was not truly a mother.

The importance of a mother cannot be overstated.

Abraham Lincoln said, "All that I am or hope to be, I owe to my angel mother."[3] George Washington said, "The greatest teacher I ever had was my mother."[4] Sir Winston Churchill said, "If we want to change our nation, begin by enlisting the mothers."[5] Napoleon Bonaparte said, "The future destiny of the child is always the work of the mother."[6] I believe testimonials like these are the rule not the exception.

For example, in the book of II Kings, when a new king is introduced, usually his mother will be mentioned.

> II Kings 14:2 "his mother's name was"
> II Kings 15:2 "his mother's name was"
> II Kings 18:2 "his mother's name was"
> II Kings 21:1 "his mother's name was"
> II Kings 22:1 "his mother's name was"
> II Kings 23:31 "his mother's name was"
> II Kings 23:36 "his mother's name was"
> II Kings 24:8 "his mother's name was"
> II Kings 24:18 "his mother's name was"

I don't believe genealogy was the reason for the mother's name being included. It was confirming the influence of the mother. Some had a good influence and others had a bad influence on the king. This influence is not just observed in the Bible.

> Sir Walter Scott's mother was a superior woman, well educated, and a great lover of poetry and painting. Byron's mother was proud, ill tempered, and violent. The mother of Napoleon Bonaparte was noted for her beauty and energy. Lord Bacon's mother was a woman of superior mind and deep piety. The mother of Nero was a murderess. The mother

of Washington was pious, pure, and true. The
mother of Patrick Henry was marked by her
superior conversational powers. The mother of
John Wesley was remarkable for her
intelligence, piety, and executive ability, so
that she has been called "the mother of
Methodism." It will be observed that in each of
these examples the sons inherited the
prominent traits of the mother.[7]

The influence of these mothers was unmistakable and
enormous. Today is no exception. We can find mothers that
have a good influence on the child and mothers that have a
bad influence on the child. One thing is certain, a mother will
influence.

The Bible points out the importance of a mother. Sarah,
Rebekah, Rachel, Ruth, and Hannah are just a few examples in
Scripture. In addition, some of the most familiar verses in the
Bible point to the importance of a mother.

For God so loved the world that he gave His
only begotten Son, that whosoever believeth in
him should not perish, but have everlasting
life. For God sent not his Son into the world to
condemn the world but that the world through
him might be saved (John 3:16-17 KJV).

You may say, "I don't see one word about a mother in that
verse." That is true in one respect. I realize that Jesus was sent
that "the world through Him might be saved." If we think
about God sending His Son into the world, we should also
think of who Jesus was entrusted to. Mary found favor with
God. Scripture shows us a young woman who was not

superhuman. She did not understand how the Messiah could be conceived in her womb. "How shall this be, seeing I know not a man?" (Luke 1:34 KJV). Yet she was a person of great faith. She may not have understood how this could happen, but she believed it would. Mary confirmed this belief when she said, "Behold the handmaid of the Lord; be it unto me according to thy word" (Luke 1:38 KJV). Months later, we see Mary praising the Lord. Just as the angel had proclaimed, she brought forth a son, and called him JESUS (Luke 1:31). Of all the people on this earth, who did God *send* Jesus to? God did not *send* Jesus to a powerful King. He did not *send* Jesus to a great military man. God did not *send* Jesus to a great theologian. God did not *send* Jesus to a priest. God Almighty placed His Son in the loving hands of a mother. A mother that watched her son Jesus grow from a baby into a young man. She watched Him be crucified at Calvary to become the Savior of the world. Mary, the mother of Jesus, was the only person that we have record of being at both Jesus' birth and His death. The love of a mother is always present. Whether you are talking about the mother of Jesus, my mother, my son's mother, your mother, or any other mother in the world, the love of a mother cannot be emphasized enough.

Jesus

Jesus certainly loved His mother. We can see His love for her during His first miracle, turning water into wine. Mary does not say, "They have no wine. Jesus, I want You to make some wine." As Jesus' mother, she knew Him better than anyone on this earth. She simply said, "They have no wine" (John 2:3b). Jesus' reply to Mary is not a rebuke "but as an indication of his willingness at the proper time to furnish wine. In all this transaction he evinced [demonstrated] the appropriate feelings of a son toward a mother."[8]

Again at Calvary, we see Jesus' love and concern for Mary.

> When Jesus therefore saw His mother, and the disciple whom He loved standing by, He said to His mother, "Woman, behold your son!" Then He said to the disciple, "Behold your mother!" And from that hour that disciple took her to his own home (John 19:26-27).
>
> Mary was poor. It would even seem that now she had no home. Jesus, in his dying moments, filled with tender regard for his mother, secured for her an adopted son, obtained for her a home, and consoled her grief by the prospect of attention from him who was the most beloved of all the apostles. What an example of filial attention! What a model to all children! And how lovely appears the dying Savior, thus remembering his afflicted mother, and making her welfare one of his last cares on the cross, and even when making atonement for the sins of the world![9]

To express His love and concern for Jerusalem, Jesus did not compare the love of a husband for his wife, or the love of a religious leader for the people, or the love of a leader for a nation. Instead, He compared the love of a mother hen for its chicks to His love and concern for Jerusalem. "O Jerusalem, Jerusalem, the one who kills the prophets and stones those who are sent to her! How often I wanted to gather your children together, as a hen gathers her chicks under her wings, but you were not willing!"(Matthew 23:37). This is one of the most touching verses in the Bible. You can almost feel the burden, the love, the concern of a mother crying out to a child that will not listen. Jesus wanted to be like a mother hen to Israel, but they refused to let Him.

Living in the country we raised chickens, and I would often watch a hen protect her young. When she thought there was danger, the hen would cluck and the baby chicks would run and get under her wings. There was no way to get to the baby chicks unless you dealt with the hen. Psalm 36:7 promises the same protection for us. "How precious is Your loving kindness, O God! Therefore the children of men put their trust under the shadow of thy wings" (Psalm 36:7 KJV).

You

The love of a mother has filled many books and could fill many more. Most of us hold fond memories of our moms. Personally, I have so many about my mom that I could write another book and the title would be "Yellow Root, Jesus and You." The book would contain some of her quotes, her experiences, and some of the old remedies my mom would "doctor" us with. I am sure you too could tell or write volumes about your mom. Many of us have run to mom crying, wanting her to make a cut or scratch well. Typically, as we grow older, we no longer run to mom. It may be because, like my mom, she has moved on to heaven.

We may not have a mom to run to, but the cuts, scratches and calamities of life still come our way. We all have someone like a mother hen that is calling out to us and compelling us to come and find refuge in the shadow of His wings.

Jerusalem was standing out in the open without the protection of God when Jesus said, "O Jerusalem, Jerusalem, the one who kills the prophets and stones those who are sent to her! How often I wanted to gather your children together, as a hen gathers her chicks under her wings, but you were not willing!"(Matthew 23:37). Jerusalem was easy prey for the enemy. Jerusalem did not run to take refuge in Jesus. Instead, they trusted in themselves. Consequently, Jerusalem was destroyed in A.D. 70 by the Roman General Titus. During the destruction of the city, not one stone of the temple was left standing on another stone. Jesus had warned Jerusalem, but it was not received. Today the same warning is made to us. The following illustration will help us understand.

> Once when Alexander the Great laid siege to a city, he had a great lamp set up, and he kept it burning night and day as a signal to the besieged. He sent word to the people in the city that while the lamp was burning, they had time to save themselves by surrender. But once the lamp was put out, the city and all that were in it would be destroyed without mercy. So God has set up His light, the cross, and waits year after year, inviting people to come to Him that they might have light and salvation. Will you exhaust His patience until it is too late? Remember what happened to Jerusalem! Redeem the time![10]

Mothers, Jesus and You. Jesus is still calling. Like a mother that sees destruction ahead for her child, He is calling you. He wants to gather you under His wing. He wants to protect you from the enemy. The question is - will you let Him?

Chapter 8: Opportunities, Jesus and You

"Today's opportunity is yesterday's dream and tomorrow's memory."[1]

Opportunities

When Donna and I got married, I was trying to finish college and work the evening shift at a local company. To avoid a student loan, we were paying tuition each semester. We had little debt but even less money. We both had old used cars. Donna was a super saver when it came to groceries. We didn't eat out. As a matter of fact, we ate so many grilled cheese sandwiches that it took years for me to regain my taste for them. We didn't have a lot of free time during the week, but we would eat some weekend meals with our parents when possible. We lived in a very small, used mobile home. It had about 700 square feet of living space. It had two bedrooms, but one was so small it should have been called a walk-in closet. I was continually doing repairs on it. For example, the heating element in the little hot water heater that was located under the kitchen sink would only last for a couple of months at a time. I became an expert at replacing that element.

About a year into our marriage, Donna was diagnosed with rheumatic fever and was restricted to total bed rest. I was still going to school and working, so for her to get the rest she needed, we moved in with her mom and dad. (Let me say this before I continue, I could not have asked for better in-laws. They loved me like a son, and they did have better meals.) The doctor had told us it would be about three months before Donna could start getting back to her normal routine. Notice I said "start." Full recovery would be longer. Meanwhile, the medical bills made the financial situation worse. During her recovery, I asked God for a new job. I needed one that paid more. I really didn't ask for a job that had better working conditions or better benefits. I just needed a job that paid more, and one that I could work and continue going to school. About two or three weeks after I prayed for the new job, I got laid off from my existing job. You may have never experienced such answers to your prayers, but that was a shock to me. I must have prayed something wrong. I had a communication problem. I wanted a *new* job, not *no* job. I could definitely relate to the members of the following congregation.

> In a church in the Deep South the preacher was moving toward the end of his sermon, and with growing crescendo he said, "This church, like the crippled man, has got to get up and walk." And the congregation responded, "That's right, reverend, let it walk." And he added, "This church, like Elijah on Mount Carmel, has got to run." "Run, let it run, preacher. Let it run." "This church has got to mount up on wings like eagles and fly." "Let it fly, preacher. Let it fly." Then he added, "Now if this church is

gonna fly, it's gonna take money." "Let it
walk, preacher. Let it walk. Let it walk."[2]

If anything was "gonna" take money, we were in trouble.
But looking back, those years hold fond memories of growing
to love each other more and more and growing to love and
appreciate others. I will never forget when some of the
members of Whites Chapel Baptist Church where we were
members brought us enough money to pay our mobile home
payment. It wasn't a large payment, but when Aunt Annie and
Uncle Ira and others gave it to us, it was like a million dollars.
What's more, God did answer my prayer and provided a job.
And over the last thirty-plus years, we have been blessed
"exceedingly abundantly above all that we ask or think,
according to the power that works in us" (Ephesians 3:20)
because of that particular job.

During the first three years of our marriage, some
unbelievable opportunities came our way, but we just couldn't
afford them. For example, we wanted to purchase a house. An
older couple that we knew in the community had decided to
move. The home was small, but it was much larger than our
mobile home and was in very good condition. In addition, it
was located on over four acres of land. After looking at the
home and talking to this wonderful couple, they told us they
had decided to sell it to us for $8,000! It was perfect for us and
the price was unbelievable! *But* there was a problem. Eight
thousand dollars was like eight million to us. We simply could
not come up with the money to pay for it. This opportunity
was lost. "The ancient Greeks had a statue called *Opportunity*.
It stood on its toes to show how quickly it might pass by. It
had wavy hair in the front that people might grasp it by the
forelock, but it was bald in back to show that when it had once
passed, it could not be caught."[3] In regards to the house, all we
could do was to watch the back of a bald head go by.

75

Looking back over the years, I have lost a lot of opportunities simply because I did not grasp the wavy hair in front. I could have, but I didn't. One such instance was an opportunity to purchase stock of a company that I thought was not going to do very well. Contrary to my belief, the stock doubled in value in the next couple of months. I could give you a lot more of my examples, but I am sure you have experienced the same in your life.

You and I are not by ourselves when it comes to missed opportunities. In his book *Life Wide Open*, Dr. David Jeremiah tells the following story of an opportunity that was lost not because the person couldn't but because the person didn't.

> Walter invited his good friend Arthur to take a ride with him out into the country. They drove past groves of fruit trees and dilapidated shacks to an area that looked to Arthur like a barren wasteland. Walter began telling his friend about the exciting plans he had for this boring parcel of land southeast of downtown Los Angeles, California. Walter's express purpose was to give Arthur the opportunity to become an investor in his dream.
>
> Walter had enough money for his main project, but he wanted to ensure that the land surrounding his venture would be bought up at the same time. He was confident that within five years the whole area would be filled with hotels, restaurants, and even a convention center serving the throngs of people who came to visit his development.
>
> But Walter's friend, radio and television personality Art Linkletter, could not see the

potential and turned down the opportunity to buy up the acres and acres of land that now surround Disneyland, the dream of his friend, Walt Disney. Today that "barren wasteland" in Orange County, California, is worth billions of dollars.[4]

Not all opportunities are as great as this. As a matter of fact, some opportunities are not good at all. You may have the opportunity to advance in your company and get a huge salary increase, but if your family is going to suffer because of the promotion, the opportunity would not be good. So we cannot categorize all opportunities as good. In fact, some opportunities are criminal. Every time you drive by a bank, you have the opportunity to rob it. Every time you drive on the interstate, you have the opportunity to go a 100 mph if your car will go that fast. For our discussion, I would like to focus on good opportunities that were lost because individuals "did not" take advantage of them.

We don't have to look far to find plenty of examples of others who have experienced lost opportunities. Some of the greatest lost opportunities are found in the Bible. For example, the people that didn't listen to Noah lost the opportunity to enter the Ark and drowned. The children of Israel did not believe Joshua and Caleb, but they believed the other spies. As a result, the children of Israel lost the opportunity to go into the Promised Land and wandered in the wilderness for forty years. The rich young ruler refused to follow Jesus and went away sorrowful. One thief on the cross didn't take advantage of the forgiveness Jesus offered while the other thief did. They all lost these opportunities because they "would not."

Peter and the other disciples had some of the greatest opportunities that have ever been offered to mankind. The disciples had been taught by Jesus for three years to look for

Jesus' death, burial, and resurrection. They had the knowledge of the resurrection before it happened. They could have been the first at the tomb to confirm the resurrection and the first to proclaim the gospel of Jesus Christ. However, when this opportunity came, the disciples were just wondering what to do next. Instead, it was the women who went to the tomb and our Lord first appeared to. It was the women who first proclaimed the gospel and experienced the excitement of carrying the message, "He is risen!" Not only did the disciples fail to take advantage of the opportunity to be the first to proclaim the good news, they failed to be the first to believe the resurrection of Christ was true.

> They left the tomb and broke the news of all this to the Eleven and the rest. Mary Magdalene, Joanna, Mary the mother of James, and the other women with them kept telling these things to the apostles, but the apostles didn't believe a word of it, thought they were making it all up (Luke 24:10-11MSG).

The disciples had the opportunities available to them, but they did not seize the opportunities because they "would not."

Jesus

After the resurrection Jesus showed Himself to the disciples. "After these things Jesus showed himself again to the disciples at the sea of Tiberias" (John 21:1). Jesus was waiting on the shore where He had prepared breakfast for them. Most sermons and lessons from this passage will focus on the conversation between Jesus and Peter, and this is certainly important to be understood. But I would like for us to consider what the disciples might have been thinking while they were listening to Jesus. The thoughts of the disciples could have been on their unbelief or the lost opportunity that any one of them could have been the one to go to the tomb that morning. If that was what they were thinking, the opportunity was gone. Nonetheless, just because one opportunity was lost did not put an end to all the opportunities that Jesus had in store for them. He was not reminding them of the past. He was pointing them to the future. He was giving them an even greater opportunity when He later said:

> Go therefore and make disciples of all the nations, baptizing them in the name of the Father and of the Son and of the Holy Spirit, teaching them to observe all things that I have commanded you; and lo, I am with you always, *even* to the end of the age. Amen (Matthew 28:19-20).

You

Opportunities, Jesus and You. All of us have experienced the loss of good opportunities. If we dwell on the lost opportunities, we will always live in the past. If the disciples had continued to live in the past with all their regrets and what-ifs, they would have had little to no effect on history. Instead, they took hold of the opportunities that lay ahead of them and the Holy Spirit used them to spread the good news to the world.

What Jesus did for Peter and the disciples, He is willing to do for you. "For there is no partiality with God" (Romans 2:11). Just because you have totally failed to grasp a good opportunity does not mean you will never have another opportunity. "Failure is the opportunity to begin again, more intelligently."[5] The disciples learned from their missed opportunities. After being with the resurrected Christ, the disciples were changed. No longer were they hiding in a room wondering what was going to happen to them. Instead, they were on the front lines spreading the gospel. Jesus gave them a new opportunity. The disciples made the decision not to lose that opportunity. As a result, their lives were totally changed and so was the world around them.

But you know what the disciples did. The question is, "What are you going to do?" "Many do with opportunities as children do at the seashore: They fill their little hands with sand, and then let the grains fall through, one by one, till all are gone."[6] As Jesus places opportunities in your hand each day, remember "God does not hold us responsible for opportunities we do not have. However, He does hold us responsible for the ones we do have."[7]

Don't be like the disciples and let someone else receive the blessings and the joy that you could have. Quit living with the regrets of the past. Instead, grasp the opportunities of today and the future.

Chapter 9: TV, Movies, Jesus and You

"We are bathed in information until we no longer feel its force."[1]

TV and Movies

I have noticed over the years that the content of TV programs, the news, and movies has become more graphic, gory, violent, brutal, provocative, confrontational, and whatever other word you would like to add.

For example, the language, nudity, sex and violence in a movie or TV program seem to be more important than a good story. It is often hard to find a good movie or TV program to watch. The Motion Picture Association of America (MPAA) ratings and the TV Parental Guidelines mean nothing. I shouldn't say, "They mean nothing." They mean nothing to me because I don't trust their judgment, but they mean something to the companies, producers, etc. They want a PG13 rating or higher in order to make the show or movie draw more viewers. At one time movies were not rated, but eventually, due to the content, ratings were required. Now TV programs are rated, and as I see some commercials, I am convinced they need to be rated too.

When it comes to the news, it is not uncommon to see the blood or bodies of soldiers that have been ambushed or killed. On the same news cast, you may see a child injured in a school bus wreck, the devastation of an earthquake, or a hurricane or tornado. You may see the bodies of a mass execution by a drug cartel. In just thirty minutes of "news" you can hear or see things that seem to be from a fictional movie. Surely, this is not real life, but all of this is real to someone.

Society as a whole has become numb to reality. All the blood, violence, crude language, nudity, and sensuality are just part of life to some. Just like a movie, the events seem real, but at the same time they are at a distance. For someone watching Hurricane Katrina on the news, it may look like a disaster movie. But if you were standing on a bridge or on top of your home or in some other way crying out for help in New Orleans, it was real. All the horrors of war on TV every day numbs the viewer to the mental and physical pain the war causes. Or, it is just another health report about aging unless you are watching a loved one going through the terrible battle of Alzheimer's. When we see and hear all the "real" and "unreal" information, it becomes hard to relate or empathize or distinguish in our mind between what is real and what is not real because we see so much of it. We become desensitized. We are at a distance from the situation. For example, if you were watching a house float down a river on TV, your sense of loss may be the same whether it was a movie or the news. You would probably be amazed at the force of the water. However, if it were your house that was floating down the river, your thoughts would be on the "home" not the "house." If you were watching a news report or a TV show about a company on the verge of going out of business, your feelings may be thoughts of the economy in general. But if it were the company you worked for, your thoughts would be on your family. If you were watching a movie or the news and both contained footage of a flag draped coffin being removed from an aircraft, you may be thinking of the success of the war or the necessity of the war. But if you were the mother of that soldier, your thoughts would be on the son or daughter who you had held as a child and watched grow into a young man or woman.

Over the years, I have been guilty of watching the news from a distance. I knew it was real, but it didn't affect me. It was like watching a movie. Needless to say, most of us have been guilty of this. Also, over the years I have been "in the movie." The things that happened affected me. There is a lot of difference between "watching a movie" and "being in the movie." For example, I remember when my father-in-law and my "Poppie" went on to be with the Lord. If you were reading their obituaries in the newspaper, you would see the names Jack L. Callaway or Edward Cameron. You may or may not have known either one of them. If you did know them and read the obituary, it would have said very little about these wonderful men. But to me, the entire newspaper could not report all the fun and wonderful memories of these two men – laughing, drinking coffee, playing cards and enjoying the grandchildren. For those of you that didn't know them, it would be just an obituary.

In the years that God has allowed me to be here, I have been in many "movies." For example, the following story would have been just another story if seen on a news report, but to me it was a story that had major effects on my life. It all began one morning at breakfast. While drinking coffee, Donna said, "I need to tell you something. Last night, the Lord woke me up and told me to check my breast." You would have to know Donna to understand the shock I felt when she told me what had happened. Donna is a wonderful Christian woman.

During our forty-two years of marriage, I have watched her study God's Word and be such a wonderful mother to our sons and a servant to the Lord. I could not ask for a better wife and friend. I have often heard her say, "God made me aware of something through His Word," but I had never heard her say God had spoken to her like this. Please don't get me wrong; I believe God can and does speak to individuals in various ways. He is sovereign. He is in control. He has never called me at any time of the day to ask my opinion. But Donna had never, ever said anything like this to me. With that said, let me continue to tell you about the "movie" that we were in.

She continued, "I got up and did what I was told. When I did, I found a lump in my breast." I could not believe what I was hearing. Donna had always been faithful about getting her mammograms each year. That past year she had been so busy as a pastor's wife and with other activities that the yearly mammogram had slipped by. Again let me say, I had never heard Donna say the Lord had spoken to her in this manner. I just wanted to believe she was wrong. I asked if she were sure. Her answer was "Yes."

We knew a doctor's appointment should be made as soon as possible. I was praying that God would command the lump to be gone and no lump would be found. Meanwhile, the Lord provided an appointment with Dr. Morris that day. Dr. Morris is a wonderful doctor and Christian. He is excellent in diagnosing any aliment, and he has a wonderful sense of humor. This time was different. He found the lump and immediately talked about the situation, suggesting Donna see a surgeon as soon as possible. With the help of Dr. Morris, Donna was referred to Dr. Pennington the next day - Friday. Dr. Pennington did a biopsy and discussed the possibilities with us. Through the weekend and into Monday, we prayed the biopsy would not be malignant. We cried, hugged and prayed more. The following Tuesday, Dr. Pennington's office called and asked if we could meet with him to discuss the biopsy. I will never forget that meeting. Sitting at a conference table with Donna, Joey (our oldest son) and me, Dr. Pennington, an outstanding surgeon and a believer, in his soft spoken voice said, "Mrs. Rich, your biopsy came back and it was positive." Then he continued to inform us of the type of cancer saying that it was very aggressive. He then explained the options that were available. At that point, whether we liked it or not, we no longer were "watching the movie." We, especially Donna, were in it. The news was not a TV medical report that would be forgotten in a few minutes. It was real and personal.

After much prayer, Donna decided to go ahead with surgery as soon as possible. Her attitude concerning the cancer will always be one of the greatest sermons that I have ever heard. She was confident that the Lord would receive glory from all of this. With that trust, the surgery was performed about two weeks after the biopsy. The news was encouraging – the cancer had not spread to the lymph nodes – but an oncologist prescribed at least ten treatments of chemotherapy. During those treatments, seven different types of chemo were used. One was so strong she had to be admitted to the hospital. Her immune system was so low she was allowed no visitors. After about six months, she was on the road to recovery and we give God all the glory. If this had been a movie, it would have been a love story and a story about the grace and mercy of God. It was not fiction, but a true life story, and we were in the "movie."

Jesus

Like the "Preview of Coming Attractions" at a theater, Jesus spoke of what the disciples should expect.

> I've told you these things to prepare you for rough times ahead. They are going to throw you out of the meeting places. There will even come a time when anyone who kills you will think he's doing God a favor. They will do these things because they never really understood the Father. I've told you these things so that when the time comes and they start in on you, you'll be well-warned and ready for them (John 16:1-4a MSG).

But we must remember Jesus' words apply to us as well. As believers, we will be in the "movie," and our part will involve suffering at some time. The "movie" from an earthly view, may not end with the hero riding off into the sunset with the girl of his dreams. As A. W. Tozer wrote:

> We forget that our Lord was a Man of sorrow and acquainted with grief. We forget the arrows of grief and pain which went through the heart of Jesus' mother, Mary. We forget that all of the apostles except John died a martyr's death. We forget that there were 13 million Christians slain during the first two generations of the Christian era. We forget that they languished in prison, that they were starved, were thrown over cliffs, were fed to

the lions, were drowned, that they were sewn in sacks and thrown into the ocean...[2]

We are not exempt from being "in the movie." We are not exempt from suffering. As a matter of fact, Jesus said, "I have told you all this so that you may have peace in me. Here on earth you will have many trials and sorrows. But take heart, because I have overcome the world" (John 16:33 NLT). Notice, Jesus did not say "we may" have trials and sorrows, but He said, we "will have" trials and sorrows.

Not only did Jesus speak of the "coming attractions" in the believer's life, but He also spoke of the "coming attractions" in His life. "And He [Jesus] began to teach them that the Son of Man must suffer many things, and be rejected by the elders and chief priests and scribes, and be killed, and after three days rise again" (Mark 8:31).

Certainly, Jesus can empathize with us when we are "in the movie," instead of just watching. As Jesus prayed in Gethsemane, we see Him wanting "this cup" be removed from His life.

> And He was withdrawn from them about a stone's throw, and He knelt down and prayed, saying, "Father, if it is Your will, take this cup away from Me; nevertheless not My will, but Yours, be done." Then an angel appeared to Him from heaven, strengthening Him. And being in agony, He prayed more earnestly. Then His sweat became like great drops of blood falling down to the ground (Luke 22:41-44).

"This cup" was worse than all the cancer, sorrow, loneliness, pain, guilt, disease, blindness, sickness and anything else that can attack an individual. But notice, He added, "nevertheless not My will, but Yours, be done" (Luke 22:42b).

> Jesus was not wrestling with God's will or resisting God's will. He was yielding Himself to God's will. As perfect Man, he felt the awful burden of sin, and His holy soul was repelled by it. Yet, as the Son of God, He knew that this was His mission in the world.[3]

There is absolutely no possible way any human being could begin to understand or feel what Jesus was going through. And "this cup" was not taken away.

You

The Apostle Paul said he wanted "to know Him [Christ] and the power of His resurrection, and the fellowship of His sufferings, being conformed to His death" (Philippians 3:10). Paul's willingness to suffer for Jesus' sake has influenced millions. Some Christians seem to think everything will be wonderful once they accept Christ as their Savior. A. W. Tozer warned of that mindset when he wrote:

> We are all idealists. We picture to ourselves a life on earth completely free from every hindrance, a kind of spiritual Utopia where we can always control events, where we can move about as favorites of heaven, adjusting circumstances to suit ourselves. This we feel would be quite compatible with the life

of faith and in keeping with the privileged place we hold as children of God.

In thinking thus we simply misplace ourselves; we mistake earth for heaven and expect conditions here below which can never be realized till we reach the world above. While we live we may expect troubles, and plenty of them. We are never promised a life without problems as long as we remain among fallen men.[4]

If there is to be no pain, no sorrow, no tribulations, etc. in our lives, then why did Christ promise a Comforter? We need a Comforter because we hurt, cry, are lonely, and have all kinds of problems and sorrows. We cry out like Christ did, "Father, if it is Your will, take this cup away from Me; nevertheless not My will, but Yours, be done" (Luke 22:42).

It may not be today, tomorrow, next week or next year, but one thing is certain, you will be "in the movie" one day. You won't just be watching from a distance. You may be the star or in a supporting role, but someday you will be "in the movie." You may pray to God to remove the lump or to bring a wayward child home or to do away with your loneliness or to take away an addiction or some other suffering. In all likelihood, you will have your own idea of how your prayer should be answered, but don't count on God doing things your way. God is sovereign. His ways are not our ways.

Are you in "your movie" today? Is your movie a disaster movie, or a horror movie, or heartbreaking love story or something else? Are you the star? Are you in a supporting role? Will you give all the glory to God? Will you say, "Your will be done."

People are watching. Many will watch "your movie" that have never read THE BOOK. As I said at the beginning of this chapter, people have become desensitized with all the news, movies, TV, etc. It has become harder to relate or empathize or distinguish in our mind between what is real and what is not real because we see so much. However, "your movie" can make a difference. People who are watching want to know if it is really true what Jesus said, "I will never leave you, nor forsake you" (Hebrews 13:5). They want to see how "your movie" ends.

Chapter 10: Memories, Jesus and You

*"Memory is the diary
we all carry around with us"[1]*

Memories

"Memory is the diary we all carry around with us." And I would like to add, the older I get, the pages of my diary have become more and more filled with the memories of days gone by.

For me, a special time for memories has always been Christmas. It is a time to celebrate our Lord's birth and to sing praises to our Savior. It is a time for family. It is a time to watch children play with their toys or the boxes they came in. It's a time when memories are made and when memories are brought back to life in the mind - memories that bring tears to our eyes or laughter to our soul or both. I have some wonderful memories of church Christmas plays, especially the ones our sons were in. I will always remember our sons getting up early Christmas morning and searching for their gifts. I remember smelling all the wonderful food being cooked and playing games with the family. Some things became a tradition, like playing Battleship on Christmas morning. Even after Joey and Matt were married, during their Christmas visits back home, we would always play at least a game or two. But time changes things. The Battleship game stayed in the cabinet this year, but the memories brought the game out just the same - memories that will last a lifetime.

It seems in our busy, rush-rush, and hectic world, people are primarily interested and concerned about the present – today, this hour, this minute, this second. I certainly have been guilty of this lifestyle. My photos and memories would be evidence enough to find me guilty of this mindset. A few photos are framed and others (whether on paper, a disc, a flash drive, etc.) are put in photo albums or storage boxes. Memories are stored in some compartment in the brain. Both are seldom thought of unless something happens and we take time to look back and pull out the photo or the memory from storage.

For example, some of this book was written while my mom was in the hospital. As she slept, I thought of some wonderful memories I had of her and some of the memories she had shared with our family. There was no doubt about her love for the Lord, her family and Prescott Baptist Church where she had been a charter member for over sixty years. Even though she has been taken off the roll of the church, I will always have wonderful memories of her in that church.

I remember some of the Christmas plays from years ago when I was growing up. I will always hold dear that small, country church in Prescott with its beautiful, varnished pine planks covering the walls. The community was rural and poor and so was the church. When it was time for our Christmas program, just like every church in our area we had to use what we had. We certainly didn't have a big stage, a sound system, costumes or a lighting system. Don't get me wrong, there is nothing wrong with having all those things as long as it is used to *give* praise to Him and not to *receive* praise from men. I am sure our folks would have loved to have had all those things, but we couldn't afford them. Besides, we probably couldn't have gotten all that equipment in the church.

We just made do with what we had. I can remember it just like it was yesterday. At the front of the "stage" there were two eye bolts screwed into the walls on either side of the church.   Each year the women would make the "stage curtains" (or repair the ones from the previous year). Usually, they were made from white bed sheets. Next, the "curtain rings" (usually large safety pins) were attached to the top of the curtains. A wire was then placed through the eye of the safety pins allowing the curtain to be pulled back and forth with ease. With the wire stretched from one eye bolt to the other, we had our "stage curtains."

Most of the community would turn out to see the play, especially the relatives of the children. One scene that I will always remember was when the angel of the Lord told the good news to the shepherds. More often than not, the loud mouth kid got the part to say "Fear not; for, behold, I bring you good tidings of great joy, which shall be to all people" (Luke 2:10 KJV). The two most coveted roles were Mary and Joseph. With a narrator reading from Luke, an empty homemade manger, and Mary holding a doll in her arms with Joseph standing next to her, the scene was heavenly in its own way. The wise men always had the fanciest costumes and the gifts looked, as they should, like gifts for a king. As a youngster, I wasn't concerned about the age of Jesus when the wise men came, and I didn't care if three or four or fifty wise men came. I just enjoyed the play.

But just like the tradition of playing Battleship, certain things change, including my observations of Christmas. I still can't tell you how old Jesus was when the wise men came.

Nor can I tell you the number of wise men that visited the Christ child. Scripture does not give us those answers. But I do believe the wise men played a greater role than what I could have imagined. My childhood Christmas memories focused only on the birth and the events surrounding Jesus' birth. Now I look at Jesus' time on earth more as a whole instead of in segments. For example, as a youngster, the wise men were simply men wearing fancy clothes giving baby Jesus gifts. Today, I believe they were men that were used of God for a specific purpose.

We know that when the wise men made their visit that Jesus was no longer a baby in a manger. Some believe that Jesus could have been one or two years old when the wise men came to the house and gave their gifts. Scripture does not tell us Jesus' age at the time of their visit but it does tell us the family was now living in a house and that Jesus was presented gifts. "And when they had come into the house, they saw the young Child with Mary His mother, and fell down, and worshiped Him. And when they had opened their treasures, they presented gifts to Him: gold, frankincense, and myrrh" (Matthew 2:11). Years ago, I looked at the gifts as just pretty gifts, but I no longer see them that way. Instead, I see the gifts in a more practical way. I see the gifts as God's way to provide a young couple with the necessities of life. Let me explain.

In Matthew chapter 2, we read that King Herod had heard of this new king that was born in Bethlehem and he wanted Him killed. To accomplish this, he ordered all male children from two years and under to be killed. Before the order was carried out, God warned Joseph about the plan, appearing to him in a dream and saying, "Arise, take the young Child and His mother, flee to Egypt, and stay there until I bring you word; for Herod will seek the young Child to destroy Him" (Matthew 2:13). When I read that after the wise men departed that Joseph was told by the angel of the Lord to arise and flee, I can just imagine the possible sequence of events. The wise men made their visit and presented the gifts to Jesus and then they left. Mary and Joseph rejoiced and praised God. They went to bed with no idea that things were about to change. During the night, Joseph was told to go to Egypt. He was obedient. "When he arose, he took the young Child and His mother by night and departed for Egypt" (Matthew 2:14). Joseph did not wait until morning; he left immediately. He could have made excuses. Maybe they had been there a year or two and Joseph had a thriving business. He may have had all types of thoughts going through his head. "I haven't collected for the work I did on Mr. Jones cart; I am supposed to build a table for Mrs. Smith; I have Mr. Brown's door in my shop." We don't know the thoughts he had. We do know he left immediately. They did not have time to tell all of their friends goodbye. They grabbed what they could and left, but when they left, they did not leave empty handed. I believe God had used the wise men to give their gifts to use for travel and to provide for the family. God was never worried about Herod's plan. The travel plans of when to leave, where to go, how long to stay, and the funds to take care of the trip had been put in place before the earth was formed.

Scripture tells us that after the shepherds' visit "Mary kept all these things, and pondered them in her heart" (Luke 2:19). I also believe Mary kept and pondered this incredible memory about the night the wise men came and brought gifts and how they had to flee to Egypt. What's more, I believe Mary shared these and many more of these memories with Jesus. After all, memories are to be shared not stuffed in a book to be thrown away. As I think of memories in that manner, memories become more than just fond thoughts of the past. For Christians, memories are experiences of the past that have a profound effect on each of us and on generations to come. In

Christian teacher and author Dr. Bruce Wilkinson's excellent study, *The Three Chairs,* he uses three chairs and the people that sit in them to illustrate how our commitment to Christ can be affected by experiences in life.

First chair people have "firsthand knowledge and experience of God at work in their midst. People with firsthand faith, who sit in the first chair, know God, love God and have personally experienced the mighty works of God."[2]

Second chair people "knew about the mighty works of God...but they had not experienced them at the same level for themselves... They are content to sit in the second chair and observe their parents' faith rather than move to the first chair and experience God's works for themselves."[3]

Third chair people "when their parents told them stories about their grandparents, maybe the children asked about the parents' stories and about how God was working in their lives. The parents had no personal stories to tell. Over time they may have stopped telling the stories out of embarrassment for not having any miracles in their own lives... Instead of witnessing firsthand faith, they hear ancient stories that lead them to believe they are hearing about a dated, outmoded religion that cannot have meaning today in their own lives. They don't see enough to cause them to value the faith of their fathers, and so they choose not to believe."[4]

I have taught and been a student of this great study. However, as I read these statements this time, I realized that first chair people have memories of *personally* experiencing the mighty works of God. Second chair people have memories of *someone else* experiencing the mighty works of God, but no personal experiences of their own to remember. Third chair people have memories of *no one* experiencing the mighty works of God but hear of "a dated, outmoded religion that cannot have meaning today in their own lives." Then I thought of Mary. She was a first chair person. She had memories of personally experiencing the mighty works of God in her life.

Jesus

Mary wasn't the only person to have memories. Prior to Jesus' death, many memories were made of Him meeting the needs of people. Some had seen the demonic healed (Mark 1:23-26), the widow's son raised to life (Luke 7:12-15), the leper healed (Matthew 8:2-3), the paralytic healed (Luke 5:18-25), five thousand fed (John 6:5-13), and the withered hand healed (Mark 3:1-5). The disciples had memories of Jesus commanding a great storm to be still (Mark 4:37-41), feeding four thousand with seven loaves of bread and a few little fishes (Matthew 15: 32-38), and the way Jesus met a financial need when he told Peter, "Nevertheless, lest we offend them, go to the sea, cast in a hook, and take the fish that comes up first. And when you have opened its mouth, you will find a piece of money; take that and give it to them for Me and you" (Matthew 17:27). After Jesus' resurrection, many more memories were made including His appearance to five hundred at one time (I Corinthians 15:6), and His ascension into heaven (Luke 24:51). The list of memories about Jesus could go on and on. As John wrote, "And there are also many other things that Jesus did, which if they were written one by one, I suppose that even the world itself could not contain the books that would be written" (John 21:25).

Certainly, each of these miracles would be a memory for those individuals, but we must remember that Jesus taught Christians to be instruments that He can use to meet the needs of others.

> For I was hungry and you gave me something to eat, I was thirsty and you gave me something to drink, I was a stranger and you invited me in, I needed clothes and you clothed me, I was sick and you looked after me, I was in prison and you came to visit me...whatever you did for one of the least of these brothers and sisters of mine, you did for me (Matthew 25:35-36, 40 NIV).

In these verses, Jesus is making it clear that the needs of others should be met by believers. When Christians are obedient to Christ's instructions, the person whose need is met has personally experienced God meeting his need. He now has a memory of what God has done for him using a believer. God still meets the need with a miracle, but it is the miracle of a Christian's heart being changed and allowing Christ to use the believer to meet the need.

> Hugh Latimer in England, in the days of the Reformation, said to his large congregation, "you can build a hundred churches and fill them with gold statues and with candles as big as oaks, but if you do not love your neighbor and feed the hungry and clothe the naked, you will go to hell in spite of all."[5]

You may or may not agree with the Latimer's statement. After all, it is just a man saying some words, but you cannot disagree with what Jesus taught.

You

With the wise men, there was no great "miracle." They were men used of God to give gifts. No river was turned into blood. No water came from a rock. Rain was not stopped for three years. The wise men were used of God to simply give gifts to Jesus and they probably never knew how the gifts were used. No strings were attached. The memory of the wise men was a personal experience to Mary and the story continues to be handed down for thousands of years.

Do you have your own personal memories and experiences of God working in *your* life? Mary, the disciples and many people that you may have known personally were in the first chair, but what about you? When you are on your death bed, will you have memories of the money you made, the position/power you had, or maybe the day you were presented a gold watch? If these are all the memories you will have, you have very little written on the pages of your memory diary. They may mean something to you but will have very little significance in the future. However, if you have memories of how you were used of God to help others, these memories will live forever. The next generation will see and desire their own memories and experiences of God personally working in their lives.

As a child, I watched the Christmas play in that small, rural church and thought how great it would be to be a wise man. Little did I know or realize that I was watching a lot of "wise men and women" as they stuck safety pins through bed sheets or pulled a wire from one eye bolt to the other. They were being used by God and giving their gifts - maybe a little money, maybe their time like the ladies that worked so hard to get everything ready, or maybe their talents making the costumes for the kids. Whatever the case, they allowed me to have a personal experience of God's work and a memory to pass on to my sons.

Memories, Jesus and You. God has given all of us the opportunity to be "wise men" and "wise women" and create many memories by giving and sharing time, blessings, and most of all, the gospel with others. The world needs wise men and wise women. Will you be one? If not, don't complain when you realize your son or your daughter has no memories of God doing anything in your life, and consequently, no memories of God doing anything in theirs.

Chapter 11: Children, Jesus and You

> *"Life's aspirations come in the guise of children."*[1]

Children

Over the years, many comments have been made about children. Some of the comments are serious and some are made in jest. The following is just a few statements that illustrate the many thoughts people have had about children.

> Too much love never spoils children. Children become spoiled when we substitute "presents" for "presence."[2]
>
> Whenever a baby is born, in essence God says, "Take this child and rear him or her for me." The tragedy is that so many babies are more *damned* than *born* into the world. They are unwanted, uncared-for – left to grow up like weeds in a wilderness. Fortunate is the child and wise the parents when the parents seek and follow the guidance and will of the Lord in rearing their children.[3]

There are no illegitimate children—only illegitimate parents.[4]

Children are not so different from kites…children were created to fly. But they need wind – the undergirding and strength that come from unconditional love, encouragement, and prayer.[5]

There never was a child so lovely but his mother was not glad to see him asleep.[6]

Even more ominous than the sound of a riot is a bunch of kids suddenly quiet.[7]

The Bible speaks of children as blessings from the Lord and "children's children are the crown of old men" (Proverbs 17:6a). These "blessings" are impossible to describe. Children can make you laugh and they can make you cry. They can make you mad and make you proud. They have the ability to communicate with words that have never been spoken before. But one of the most well-known characteristics of children is their unpredictability. Children are unpredictable! Our sons have confirmed this fact many times. For example, after Matt's first day of kindergarten, Donna and I were anxious to hear all about his day. Both of us asked him questions, but the answers we received were not what we were looking for. We wanted to hear more detail not one or two word answers. For example, when we asked, "Did you enjoy school?" we wanted more than "Yes ma'am" for an answer. Or when we asked, "What did you do today?" We wanted more than "Different stuff." We asked about his best friend Tiffany who was in his class. No matter how or what we asked, his answer was polite but short. Finally, he couldn't hold it back any longer. Out of nowhere he said, "She (not Tiffany) hit me first." Well, at least we finally got more than one or two words. Needless to say, we did get more details.

Joey, our oldest son, had his moments too. One Sunday, he was about four or five years old and was sitting with us in the sanctuary at church. He had always been a well-behaved child, and we had never had any problems with him being with us in worship but that Sunday morning was different. He was misbehaving. I didn't use the "counting to three warning system." A couple of good stern looks usually corrected bad behavior. This time was an exception, so I picked him up and headed for the back door as reverently and as quietly as possible. A few steps from the door, Joey said, "Daddy, can't we just talk about this?" I have to admit, discipline was difficult when I knew everybody in the church heard his plea for mercy and would ask , "You didn't spank him, did you?"

It seems these unpredictable moments are just waiting to happen when children are at church or with church folks. For example, the following is one of those unpredictable, "crawl in a hole," moments that I read about.

> My wife was busy one evening pursuing her hobby of making porcelain dolls at a doll-making class, leaving me at home to watch our two children, Melinda, age seven, and Craig, age five. While I was chatting with a neighbor on the front porch, the phone rang. I was proud to hear Craig answer the phone promptly and politely. My pride vanished as I heard my son's response to the caller's request to speak to my wife: "No, my mom's not here. She's out making a baby. But my dad is here if you want to talk to him."
>
> Naturally, the phone call was from one of the elders of our church![8]

At church, a good method to teach children about thanksgiving, praise, trust, and much more is to ask if they have any prayer requests and then have a time to tell how God has blessed them. It also presents another opportunity for them to demonstrate their unpredictability. Prayers and praise can be for mom, dad, cats, dogs, school, whatever. God is interested in them all! At the end of one class, a girl volunteered to say the prayer. She prayed for various people, especially her grandfather who was the pastor, and for other concerns. Then, I guess, she wanted to give God some good advice or encouragement. She finished, "Now God, just hang in there. Amen."

Praise time was also unpredictable. During one praise time, a boy raised his hand. He had something he wanted everyone to know that he was thankful for. His uncle, an avid hunter, had just gotten a brand new rifle. There was no doubt in his mind that this had to be a miracle from God. On another occasion during Sunday school, Donna was letting the children act out the events leading up to the crucifixion. One girl of about eight years old informed all the other children that "she was going to be Jesus and they would be the people." Everything was going quite well. The other children began to act like they were crying. At that point, Wanda (playing Jesus) noticed that the "lesson" was not going according to Scripture. So with a very disgusted voice, the following corrective directions were made: "Stop that! Nobody has spit on me yet!"

The following is just one more story to help confirm the unpredictably of children:

FMC member Fr. Michael Hayduk, pastor of St. Mary's Byzantine Catholic Church in Cleveland, Ohio, visited the church's preschool and day-care center one day. A new group of little ones had started at the center, and one boy, about three years old, ask the priest, "Why do you dress funny?"

Fr. Hayduk told him he was a priest and this was the uniform that priests wear. Then the boy pointed to Hayduk's collar insert and asked: "Does that hurt? Do you have a boo-boo there?"

Hayduk took the plastic collar insert out and showed it to the boy. The name of the manufacture is embossed on the reverse side. The boy felt the letters, and the priest asked him "Do you know what those words say?"

"Yes, I do!" said the boy, who was not old enough to read. "It says, 'Kills ticks and fleas up to six months!'"[9]

Children may not always be predictable, but there is one thing that seems to be predictable concerning a child. Somewhere, sometime, and somehow, a child will be asked, "What do you want to be when you grow up?" Most all of us adults have been guilty of asking that question. But have you ever thought, "What if the child was to ask an adult the same question?" I am sure the answer from the child and the answer from the adult would be different. Same question, but different answers. This is not because of age. It is not because the adult has already grown up. I believe the answers are different because the focus of the child and the adult are different.

Let me explain. To make sure we are comparing apples to apples, I will drop the "when you grow up." As a result, the question to both the child and the adult will be, "What do you want to be?" The child will have no problem understanding this question. When the child is asked what he wants to be, he or she may answer: a nurse, a fireman, a doctor, a teacher, a baseball player, a preacher, or a race car driver. When the adult is asked the same question, he or she may say: out of debt, free from pain, in a new house or neighborhood, or to be retired. Somewhere between childhood and adulthood, the focus has changed. The focus goes from "becoming" to "wanting." With the child, the focus is on the internal. He or she wants to become a certain type of person. The adult's focus is no longer internal but external. The adult's "wants" are usually centered on things. The mindset has changed.

Jesus

During the ministry of Jesus, we can see this same difference in attitude/mindset. For example, "when the chief priests and scribes saw the wonderful things that He did, and the children crying out in the temple and saying, 'Hosanna to the Son of David!' they were indignant" (Matthew 21:15). Notice the children were focused on the internal – praising our Lord Jesus. The priests and scribes were focused on the external. They were envious of Jesus. They wanted the praise of men.

We find this mindset/attitude to be the case in many of the adults in the Bible. For example, Jesus fed "five thousand men, besides women and children" (Matthew 14:21). Another time, Jesus feed four thousand. "Now those who had eaten were about four thousand" (Mark 8:9). However, Jesus knew their motive, their mindset. Jesus said, "You've come looking for me not because you saw God in my actions but because I fed you, filled your stomachs – and for free" (John 6:26 MSG). Also, Jesus healed so many people "everyone who had something wrong was pushing and shoving to get near and touch him" (Mark 3:10b MSG). Even James and John wanted Jesus to "Grant us that we may sit, one on your right hand and the other on your left, in your glory" (Mark 10:37). All of these people wanted something external not internal. All of them would have answered the question, "What do you want to be?" with the mindset of wanting instead of becoming.

There is so much Scripture of wanting versus becoming. Scripture also gives us many examples of people that actually desired to change and "become." The woman at the well wanted water but Jesus told her, "If you knew the generosity of God and who I am, you would be asking me for a drink, and I would give you fresh, living water" (John 4:10 MSG). The woman wanted water, the external. Jesus wanted her to become a believer, the internal. After Jesus told the woman that He was the Messiah,

> ...the woman then left her water pot, went her way into the city, and said to the men, "Come, see a Man who told me all things that I ever did. Could this be the Christ?" (John 4:28-29).

The woman at the well became a believer. As a result, "many of the Samaritans of that city believed in Him because of the word of the woman who testified" (John 4:39). They believed, not because she carried water (external) back to the city, but because she carried the gospel (internal) back to the city. Notice the change of the mindset of the Samaritans. "We know [internal] that this is indeed the Christ, the Savior of the world" (John 4:42).

However, adults can seem to want to "become" and focus on the internal but it may be nothing more than concealing their real focus on wanting the external. For instance, an adult may say, "I want to become a wonderful Bible teacher." This so called desire to "become" may have been expressed in a desirable way but for the wrong reason. On the surface it appears to be a desire to have an internal change. But if the reason for wanting to become a wonderful Bible teacher is to get the praise of others, it is nothing more than a focus on the external – self recognition. Why? The person's focus is on self.

Another focus on the external is apparent when people check out churches to see what a church can offer them. Oswald Chambers, in his classic devotional *My Utmost for His Highest*, speaks of this "wanting."

> We have got so commercialized that we only go to God for something from Him, and not for Himself. It is like saying, "No, Lord, I don't want Thee, I want myself; but I want myself clean and filled with the Holy Ghost; I want to be put in Thy showroom and be able to say— 'This is what God has done for me.'" If we only give up something to God because we want more back, there is nothing of the Holy Spirit in our abandonment; it is miserable commercial self-interest.[10]

As a result, we have miserable people in our churches because we have tried to meet their external wants instead of their internal needs. "There is nothing easier than getting into a right relationship with God except when it is not God Whom you want but only what He gives."[11]

You

Children, Jesus and You. What do you want to be? As a Christian do you have a desire to become what God wants you to be? Do you have a lot of wants that nothing has satisfied?

Maybe it is time to start thinking like a child. Quit putting all the emphasis on "want" and start putting it on "be." If you are serious about this change, you will never be the same.

One good way to compare your "wanting" to "becoming" is to examine your prayers. Concerning prayer, A. W. Tozer wrote:

> Prayer among evangelical Christians is always in danger of degenerating into a glorified gold rush. Almost every book on prayer deals with the "get" element mainly. How to get things we want from God occupies most of the space. Now, we gladly admit that we may ask for and receive specific gifts and benefits in answer to prayer, but we must never forget that the highest kind of prayer is never the making of requests.[12]

God does not want to be your sugar daddy. And He won't be. He wants to be your Savior and Lord. I pray you will go to Him and pray, "Lord, I want to *become* what you want me to be and for no other reason than for you to receive the glory. Amen."

"Whether you eat or drink, or whatever you do,
do all to the glory of God."
(I Corinthians 10:31)

Chapter 12: Aunt Nell, Jochebed, Jesus and You

> *"A teacher affects eternity; he can never tell where influence stops."*[1]

Aunt Nell

I am sure you know who Jesus is and you know who you are. Do you know who Jochebed was? Do you know who Aunt Nell was? Some of you may know who Jochebed was, but many people don't. Almost none of you have any idea who Aunt Nell was. If it wasn't for being blessed with a wonderful aunt, I wouldn't be able to tell you about Aunt Nell. And if it wasn't for some Bible lessons, I wouldn't be able to tell you about Jochebeb. Hopefully, the following paragraphs will enlighten you concerning these two women.

Aunt Nell was my mother's only sister. She was younger and from birth was in very poor health. As far as I know, Aunt Nell never had any formal education, but she had a great "home school" teacher in my grandmother. Aunt Nell lived next door to us. Actually, it was more like "across the branch" from us. A small stream and a number of trees separated our homes. The distance was small. In city terms, it was less than a block away. The close proximity allowed me to go back and forth during the day. Aunt Nell always had time for me. As a preschooler, I spent many hours with her. She may have had a frail body, but God had given her a wonderful talent –she was a natural artist. She could draw and paint anything, especially flowers, landscape scenes, and animals. She could draw a horse that looked so real it looked as if it could run off the paper. There is no telling how many horses she drew for me over the years. Another of my favorite creations of hers was an animated cartoon. The cartoon was created with 120 3"x 3" flip cards. The cards had a sequence of drawings on them. Holding the cards on one side and flipping through them quickly would produce the cartoon. The funny animation showed a cat trying to catch a goldfish but ended up with the gold fish safe and the fish bowl over the cat's head. I still like to get it out and look at it or show it to someone, especially a child. My favorite work of all is the portrait she painted of Donna.

Not only could she draw, she was a wonderful and patient teacher. When I was there, she devoted a lot of time to teaching me how to draw. Looking back, I realize I failed the course. I can't draw, but I sure enjoyed every hour with her.

When I started to school, I had less time to spend with Aunt Nell, but weekends and summers provided more time to be with her. As I got older, school, dating, work, college and a family allowed less time with Aunt Nell. Now, please don't think she was just sitting around with tears in her eyes waiting to see me come through the door. She was busy with her other nephews and nieces, and I am sure they have wonderful memories of her too. Before she went on to be with the Lord, she had shared her talent and love with Donna, Joey Jr., and Matt.

Due to her health, she never married. She lived her final

years with "Poppie and Granny" (my mom and step-dad). I know she knew that I loved her very dearly as did the other members of our family. However, she probably didn't know how much she influenced me, especially with her unselfish life and vision to see the beauty in God's creation. Most of all, she taught me to appreciate art.

Jochebed

One individual in the Bible that God used to teach and influence a child adopted by a rich family was Jochebed. The adopted child was Moses, and Jochebed was the mother of Moses (Exodus 6:20a). Now just to read the previous sentences doesn't make sense. To make it even more unusual, Jocheded was paid to care for Moses. It is a very unusual situation for an adopted child to have his birth mother being paid to take care of him, but God's ways are not our ways. He is always giving bonus blessings.

This unusual relationship between mother and son was the result of events that had taken place prior to the birth of Moses. The population of the children of Israel had grown so much that the Pharaoh of Egypt regarded them as a security threat. To stop this threat, Pharaoh made them slaves, but this plan failed. To insure the reduction of the Hebrew threat, Pharaoh gave this order to his people: "Throw every newborn Hebrew boy into the Nile River. But you may let the girls live" (Exodus 1:22 NLT). It was into this setting that Moses was born.

> Now a man of the tribe of Levi married a Levite woman, and she became pregnant and gave birth to a son. When she saw that he was a fine child, she hid him for three months. But

when she could hide him no longer, she got a papyrus basket for him and coated it with tar and pitch. Then she placed the child in it and put it among the reeds along the bank of the Nile. His sister stood at a distance to see what would happen to him.

Then Pharaoh's daughter went down to the Nile to bathe, and her attendants were walking along the riverbank. She saw the basket among the reeds and sent her female slave to get it. She opened it and saw the baby. He was crying, and she felt sorry for him. "This is one of the Hebrew babies," she said.

Then his sister asked Pharaoh's daughter, "Shall I go and get one of the Hebrew women to nurse the baby for you?"

"Yes, go," she answered. So the girl went and got the baby's mother. Pharaoh's daughter said to her, "Take this baby and nurse him for me, and I will pay you." So the woman took the baby and nursed him (Exodus 2:1-9 NIV).

The exact length of time that Moses was under the direct care of Jochebed is unknown; however, there came a time when Moses became Pharaoh's daughter's adopted son. "When the child grew older, she took him to Pharaoh's daughter and he became her son. She named him Moses, saying, 'I drew him out of the water' " (Exodus 2:10 NIV).

The exact dates and length of time that Moses was under the influence of Jochebed and Pharaoh's daughter are not known, but the previous verses make it clear that two very different and conflicting ways of belief were instilled into the heart and mind of Moses.

First, the Hebrew way of thinking was instilled by

Jochebed, a woman that was a slave. The Hebrew story was the story of the Lord making a covenant with Abram (Genesis 15) and all of Abram's descendants including Isaac, Jacob, Joseph, Jochebed and Moses. It was a story that was told with conviction and love.

Next, the Egyptian way of thinking was set forth to Moses by the very best instructors of Egypt. The Egyptian story was one of power and intellect. The Egyptians instructors taught Moses about engineering, chemistry, astronomy and so many other areas of study. "Moses was learned in all the wisdom of the Egyptians, and was mighty in words and deeds" (Acts 7:22). In addition, the Egyptians could show Moses all their accomplishments. Moses could actually *experience* with his senses all that was Egypt – the pyramids, the powerful army, the slaves, the religious rites, the medicine, the hieroglyphics and much more. On the other hand, Moses could only *hear* the Hebrew story.

Moses eventually had to make a decision between these two different and conflicting ways of belief. With all that Egypt had to offer, it could not overpower the redemptive story Jochebed had taught. "By faith Moses, when he became of age, refused to be called the son of Pharaoh's daughter, choosing rather to suffer affliction with the people of God than to enjoy the passing pleasures of sin" (Hebrews 11:24-25).

Moses had to flee from Egypt when he was forty. If Jochebed was alive at that time, she may have heard about it. Maybe she never saw Moses again. Maybe she died before the children of Israel were lead out of Egypt by Moses. Maybe she never knew how much influence she had on Moses. If she didn't then, she does now.

Jesus

When it comes to influence, Jesus did not give believers the option to have or not to have influential lives. In the Sermon on the Mount, Jesus said:

> You are the salt of the earth. But if the salt loses its saltiness, how can it be made salty again? It is no longer good for anything, except to be thrown out and trampled underfoot.
>
> You are the light of the world. A town built on a hill cannot be hidden. Neither do people light a lamp and put it under a bowl. Instead they put it on its stand, and it gives light to everyone in the house. In the same way, let your light shine before others, that they may see your good deeds and glorify your Father in heaven (Matthew 5:13-16 NIV).

Notice the verses above. They are directed to "you." If you are a believer, then Jesus is speaking directly to you. You cannot interpret, change, or read, this any other way. "You are" salt and light. As a believer, being salt and light is not an option. We are to influence the world as salt influences the taste of food. We are to be a light to the world. Light makes a difference in this dark world. As a result, others will benefit by it and our Father will be glorified.

Just like Jochbed influenced Moses, so we as individuals are to influence the world around us. "You are" salt and light.

> The greatest works that have been done have been done by the ones. The hundreds do not often do much, the companies never do: it

116

is the units, just the single individuals, that, after all, are the power and the might.[2]

Your sphere may be contracted, your influence may be small: but a sphere and influence you have.[3]

You

Aunt Nell, Jochebed, Jesus and You. Aunt Nell and Jochebed were salt and light – two poor women who loved God and were willing to invest their time to be a good witness and influence to a child. How about you? There are adults and children waiting to be influenced. Are they waiting on you? You may not have a Moses to influence, but that is not for you to decide. You may not have thousands to influence but that is for God to decide. We are to obey and be influential in the area we are placed in and with the people He places in our lives. For example, our youngest son experienced such obedience and influence when he was seven years old. He was the only child in his Sunday school class; Mrs. JoAnn was his teacher. She could have said, "Let's combine classes" or made some other suggestion to avoid having a class with only one child in it. Instead, she was faithful the entire year and taught as if she had a room full. She may not know how much influence she had during that year, but some day she will.

I believe Christianity is lacking in persons of influence today. As a result, many people are in bondage of sin. Many people need to be freed from the cruel slave master known as Satan. It seems many people want to let their light shine in order to benefit themselves and to receive glory for themselves. Yet, Jesus has instructed us to do the opposite. We are to let our lights shine so that others can benefit and God will receive the glory.

Maybe what Christianity needs is more believers wanting to be a Jochebed instead of a Moses. I believe the number of leaders like Moses is directly related to the number of Jochebeds. Is God calling you to be a Jochebed – someone not in the spotlight, but willing to take time to invest in another person's life? Is a Moses waiting on you to influence him? If you are a Christian, God has placed someone in your life to influence. Maybe they are just waiting on you. Don't let your "Moses" wait any longer on you.

Chapter 13: Fingers, Jesus and You

*"If no one knows what will happen,
who can tell him when it will happen?"*
(Ecclesiastes 8:7 NASB)

Fingers

Have you ever started a morning knowing it was going to be a great day, only to have it turn out to be a disaster? I have and others have too.

For my mom, February 12, 1999, was such a day. Let me explain. For twenty-five years, Poppie (my stepdad) had been a joy and a blessing to be around. He kept us all laughing with his incredible sense of humor. The grandchildren loved his pet projects. And when I say "pet" I do mean pet. He raised rabbits, goats, chickens and quail. He loved to play card games. He probably acquired his fondness for cards during World War II while serving in the Navy. But he met his match when it came to our family. A lot of Friday nights was spent eating hamburgers and playing cards with Poppie and Granny. On a few occasions, we would "gang up" on him just to watch his face as we started laughing. I can hear him now, "Ya'll are the cheatingest bunch," or he would call Donna, who laughed the hardest, "You old heifer." I don't know how he got "old" and "heifer" together, but that was Poppie. He loved to eat, too. Not just regular meals but any time that could be made a snack time, especially with coffee. Often, after school, Donna and Matt would visit with Poppie and Granny. Granny would be expecting them and have hot homemade biscuits waiting. Of course, they would have to play a game before they left.

A lot more could be said about Poppie, but it is sufficient to say that he enjoyed life and his joy was contagious to us all. Then on February 12, 1999, while getting ready to go to a Valentine banquet at church, a massive heart attack ended the life and the laughter that we loved so much. A day Granny thought was going to be great didn't turn out that way for her.

After Poppie's death, we watched Granny (my mom) grieve. But having gone through the depression, World War II, cancer, the death of her oldest son, and more, the heartache and pain was not something new. Her faith and strength always produced praise in every situation. Instead of pity, she would talk about the blessing of having Poppie for so many years. She continued life with praise. Nevertheless, we tried to spend as much time as possible with her, especially the gloomy days of winter. We all looked forward to those occasional warm and beautiful days of winter that provided time to be outside and that lifted our spirits with the anticipation of spring around the corner.

Saturday, December 4, 1999, was such a day. The forecast was for a gorgeous day, and I knew it was going to be a great day. The morning started with the smell of Donna baking cookies. She was to teach at a ladies conference and would carry the delicious snacks with her, but I knew she would make enough to fill our cookie jar too. Saturday, perfect weather and fresh cookies, surely "this is the day the Lord hath made" and who could ask for more! I wanted to get outside and to do some landscaping work. So, I got everything ready to accomplish the task. I think even the tractor was waiting to get out too because it was running great. By this time my helper Matt was up and ready (or I should say persuaded) to join me in a great day of work.

Our first task was to move a few huge timbers next to our driveway. The creosote timbers were about 18" x 6" x 12' and very heavy. However, using the tractor, it would be somewhat easier. I would wrap the chain around the timber. Matt would use the tractor to pull the timber to the place it was needed. Then he would give me some slack on the chain to release the hook and pull the chain free. This system worked great for a while until the unexpected happened. The timber was exactly where it was needed, but my left index finger was caught in the chain. As the chain pulled free, the end of my finger was mashed. I didn't look at my finger. I just grabbed it to stop the bleeding and told Matt he would have to take me to the emergency room. I thought it had been mashed really badly and nothing more.

Donna had not left for her meeting, so I told her what had happened. She insisted on taking me, but I told her I would probably get a few stitches and be back before she would. She wanted to see the injury, but I was still squeezing it and I didn't want to let go. As a matter of fact, I felt very little pain. As Matt got his wallet and keys and I got my wallet, I convinced her to let Matt take me.

Looking back, I should have let Donna take me to the emergency room. I say this for a couple of reasons. First, I could have used some encouragement as we traveled from our home to the hospital. Instead of encouragement, Matt said, "You know dad, this could reduce the amount of time that it takes to cut your finger nails by ten percent." As his father, I quickly instructed him to be quiet and drive.

Another reason became evident at the emergency room. I had to release the strangle-hold I had on my finger in order to let the doctor make his examination. When I did, the pain level went from a two to a nine. The doctor informed me that I would need a specialist and one was on the way. Meanwhile, I was to be given an antibiotic, something for pain and a tetanus shot. When the specialist arrived, I was told that the end of the finger was severed, and I would have to have surgery immediately. They started bringing papers for me to sign, but I couldn't sign for myself because I had been given the pain medicine. Matt was not old enough to sign for me. Donna was at the meeting, so I had to get in touch with my oldest son Joey to give approval for the surgery. After that I was immediately taken to surgery, and the last thing I remembered was my hand and arm being secured as if I had some superhuman strength.

When I opened my eyes, I didn't know what was going on. I was in a hospital bed with a lot of people standing in the room. My left hand looked like a child's basketball made from gauze. I think I asked some questions, but I have no idea what they may have been. One thing was for certain, this was not the great day I had expected.

I went back to sleep and slept until the next day. When I awoke, I began to remember some of what had happened. Donna filled in the gaps. After a couple of months of therapy and lots of care from my nurse Donna, I recovered from the surgery. Without the end of my left index finger, I have had to learn how to do a lot of things differently, but that is another story. Needless to say, it has cut down on the time I have to cut my nails by ten percent. Also, most people can only count whole numbers on their fingers, but I can count fractions.

December 4, 1999, the day I knew was going to be a great day, turned out to be totally different from what I had anticipated. This was not unique to me or to my mom in February of that year. It has happened to billions of people in their own personal way. American history is filled with dates where the unexpected happened. December 7, 1941, and

September 11, 2001, are just two of hundreds of dates that are remembered. World history would add thousands more dates when the unexpected happened. "One thing the future can guarantee – anything can happen."[1] Therefore, "Do not boast about tomorrow, for you do not know what a day may bring forth" (Proverbs 27:1).

Jesus

During Jesus' ministry here on earth, He spoke often of unexpected days. For example, we see in Mark 13:1 (KJV) that when Jesus went out of the temple, one of His disciples said to him: "Master, see what manner of stones and what buildings are here!" *The Life Application New Testament Commentary* gives us some idea of what the disciples were looking at.

> The temple was impressive, covering about one-sixth of the land area of the ancient city of Jerusalem. It was not one building, but a majestic mixture of porches, colonnades, separate small edifices, and courts surrounding the Temple proper-hence the comment about the tremendous buildings...The massive stones the disciples mentioned were huge white stones, some of them measuring twenty-five by eight by twelve and weighing more than one hundred tons.[2]

Jesus' response was an unexpected one. "Do you see these great buildings? Not one stone shall be left upon another that shall not be thrown down" (Mark 13:2). Again, quoting from *The Life Application New Testament Commentary*:

Jesus made a startling statement: These magnificent buildings would be completely demolished...This happened only a few decades later when the Romans sacked Jerusalem in A.D. 70. Gazing at the massive stones, the disciples surely found it difficult to believe that not one of the stones would be left on top of another.[3]

Concerning the temple, Jesus spoke of an unexpected day in the future, and it did come to pass.

We find another example of Jesus speaking of an unexpected day (actually days) while teaching his disciples. "Jesus began to show to His disciples that He must go to Jerusalem, and suffer many things from the elders and chief priests and scribes, and be killed, and be raised the third day" (Matthew 16:21). Not expecting this statement, Peter took Jesus aside and began to rebuke him saying, "Never, Lord!" he said. "This shall never happen to you!" (Matthew 16:22 NIV). Peter and the disciples may not have believed that unexpected day would come, but it did. Later, writing to the church at Corinth, Paul would show that the unexpected days of Jesus' death, burial and resurrection would become the very core of the gospel.

Moreover, brethren, I declare to you the gospel which I preached to you, which also you received and in which you stand, by which also you are saved, if you hold fast that word which I preached to you – unless you believed in vain. For I delivered to you first of all that which I also received: that Christ died for our sins according to the Scriptures, and that He was buried, and that He rose again the third day according to the Scriptures (I Corinthians 15:1-4).

These were unexpected days that Jesus said would take place and they did. Yet, Jesus spoke a great deal about another unexpected day that has not happened yet. His return will be the most unexpected day that will ever be. Jesus said, "For as the lightning comes from the east and flashes to the west, so also will the coming of the Son of man be" (Matthew 24:27). The day has not happened yet, but it will! When it does, people will be going about their usual daily routine just as people did before Noah's flood. Jesus said,

> When the Son of Man returns, it will be like it was in Noah's day. In those days before the flood, the people were enjoying banquets and parties and weddings right up to the time Noah entered his boat. People didn't realize what was going to happen until the flood came and swept them all away. That is the way it will be when the Son of Man comes (Matthew 24:37-39 NLT).

They will be totally unaware that the unexpected will happen. For that reason, Jesus gave the following warning. "So you also must be ready, because the Son of Man will come at an hour when you do not expect him" (Matthew 24:44 NIV). It is not a matter of *if* this unexpected day will come. It *will* come! We just don't know when.

You

Have you ever had a day or week or month or even a year that you thought was going to be great but the unexpected happened? I am sure all of us have. Maybe you didn't lose the end of a finger. Maybe you have lost much more. Maybe you expected to go to college, but the unexpected happened. Maybe you expected to retire and enjoy many years with your spouse, but the unexpected happened. Maybe you expected to go visit with you parents and spend time with them, but the unexpected happened. The "Maybe you expected… but the unexpected happened" list could fill books. But the most tragic and most horrible of all the "unexpected events" will be for individuals not expecting the return of Christ. It will be too late to get ready. The following words of poet John Greenleaf Whittier ring out this warning. "For of all sad words of tongue or pen, the saddest are these: 'it might have been!'"[4] In other words, one day the unexpected day of Christ's return will happen, but the door of opportunity to get ready will be closed. A.W. Tozer helps us understand the importance of being ready:

> We have such a short time to prepare for such a long time. By that I mean we have now to prepare for then. We have an hour to prepare for eternity. To fail to prepare is an act of moral folly. For anyone to have a day given to prepare, it is an act of inexcusable folly to let anything hinder that preparation…Nothing in this world is worth it. If we believe in eternity, if we believe in God, if we believe in the eternal existence of the soul, then there is nothing important enough to cause us to commit such an act of moral folly.[5]

126

Fingers, Jesus and You. Life can only be lived one moment at a time. We never know what the next day, hour, or minute might bring. We do know that one day Jesus will return. Many people believe that day will never come. Others believe and live as if His return will be way out in the future. The issue is not what others believe, it is what do you believe. It is your decision. Jesus could return today. Are you ready for His return?

Chapter 14: Forked Tongue, Jesus and You

"Truthful words stand the test of time, but lies are soon exposed." (Proverbs 12:19 NLT)

Forked Tongue

As a young boy, I loved to watch westerns on TV, especially cowboys and Indians riding horses and fighting each other. The cowboys always won and saved the day. I still like a good western, but I have come to realize my belief about the old west was not exactly accurate. As a young boy, I thought the Indians were always the villains. Now that I am much older and hopefully wiser, I have learned the Native Americans were not always treated honorably or truthfully.

Regarding the Native Americans, General Philip Sheridan said: "We took away their country and their means of support, broke up their mode of living, their habits of life, introduced disease and decay among them, and it was for this and against this that they made war. Could anyone expect less?"[1]

"Worst of all, the government and the people showed little interest in honoring treaties made with Indians."[2] For example:

Under their mixed-blood chief, Alexander McGillivray, the Creeks turned to President Washington and negotiated a treaty which confirmed their boundaries but also acknowledged themselves to be "under the protection of the United States."... As the Creeks were to discover, neither pledge of protection nor guarantee of territory had any enduring meaning. The Indian Removal Act of 1830 swept them from their ancient homeland as if no promise had been put on paper.[3]

President Andrew Jackson wanted all the eastern tribes to "pack up and move west of the Mississippi."[4] When the Cherokees took their case to the Supreme Court, Chief Justice John Marshall affirmed the tribe's rights – but

Jackson ignored the ruling. "John Marshall has made his decision, now let him enforce it," he [President Jackson] is reputed to have said. When the Cherokees tried to withhold their consent, troops were dispatched to their homes and negotiations concluded at bayonet point. The Cherokees departed.[5]

They were forced to leave their homes and travel about a thousand miles to an Indian Territory. This deadly journey became known as the Trail of Tears. "Along the way thousands perished of hunger, cold, illness, and sorrow."[6]

The plains Indians experienced the "forked tongue" in their dealings with the government. They watched as millions of acres of land that had been designated as Indian reservations were taken from them. With the land, the buffalo, which was essential in the life of the Indian, was eliminated.

Once killed and butchered there was little the buffalo did not provide [for the Indian]. From the carcass came fresh meat for feasting and dried meat for lean times. The skin provided blankets, moccasins, mittens, shirts, leggings, dresses, and underclothes. Sinew was turned into thread and bowstrings; bones into farming tools; horns into cups, ladles, and spoons; the stomach into a water bottle. Even vanity was served. The rough side of a buffalo tongue became a hairbrush and the oily fat a plains hair tonic.[7]

By 1800 hardly any [buffalo] existed east of the Mississippi, though an estimated 40,000,000 still darkened the plains...By 1900, the nation's wild [buffalo] numbered 39 – all in Yellowstone National Park.[8]

No more efficient way could have been found for destroying the plains Indians. The disappearance of the [buffalo] left them starving, homeless, purposeless. All that remained for them was to submit to reservation life.[9]

"White man speak with forked tongue" had a lot of truth to it.

Speaking with a forked tongue is not limited to the "white man" but includes all men. The forked tongue gives everyone an equal opportunity to use it. It does not discriminate by age, ability, religion, race, gender, wealth, power, or any other category.

For some, speaking with a forked tongue, better known as lying, is a lifestyle. They may be called pathological liars, habitual liars, chronic liars or compulsive liars. Whatever term you want to use, they are addicted to lies. It is impossible to have a "normal" conversation with them. If you caught a ten pound bass, they have caught a twelve pound bass. If your doctor has diagnosed you to have three ruptured discs, the habitual liar has four. The old saying, "You can tell when he is lying when his lips move" is true for the compulsive liar.

Have you ever been lied to? "I'll pay you back next week." "This car is in excellent shape. It was owned by a little lady that only drove it to church." "The check is in the mail." Another lie that you can count on hearing is "When elected, I will..."

We have even categorized lies. The following is a great example of what some would call a "little white lie."

> Back in the days when kids traveled on trains to get somewhere with their parents, they didn't charge for kids that were five or under. And so this six-year old fellow was told by his mother, as they were carrying their bags to the train, "Tell 'em you're five." The little boy frowned and he got on the train and sat down. And the conductor came by and said, "How old are you, son?" And he says, "Ah, five." So he didn't pay anything. His mother paid her fare and the conductor left.
>
> The conductor came back a couple of hours later just to talk to him – rubbed his hand in the little fellow's hair and said, "Well, how are you gettin' along?" The boy answered, "Really good." The conductor continued their chat and said, "Let's see, when you gonna be six?" And the little boy said, "About the time I get off this train I'm gonna be six."[10]

Society encourages lying. You can hear lies everywhere. At the office, the boss tells the secretary to say, "Tell him I am out of the office right now." At home, while preparing his income tax return, the husband tells his wife, "I'm not going to report the cash that I earned last year. What the IRS doesn't know won't hurt them." Of course, the children hear his statement, and then at school the child will assure the teacher that the reading assignment has been completed when only half has been completed. After all, "What she doesn't know won't hurt her." At church, some will make a profession of faith, join the church and make a commitment to serve the Lord. Yet in two months, if that long, you couldn't find them near any church on Sunday. Also, some parents will dedicate their baby/child to God. The service is beautiful, but in reality it is a big lie. The parents will not "train up [their] child in the way he should go: and when he is old, he will not depart from it" (Proverbs 22:6). While the child is growing up, the parents show him/her the unimportance of church by their on and off attendance. The dedication was not to the Lord, it was nothing but a show. What's more, the parents continue to lie when they say, "We just don't know where we went wrong as parents. He will not listen to us. Will you visit him in jail and try to talk with him?"

Lies have become tools of choice, rather than sins to be avoided. Herschel H. Hobbs in his book, *My Favorite Illustrations,* gave the following illustration.

> A little boy was asked by his Sunday school teacher to define a lie. He said, "A lie is an abomination to the Lord, and an ever-present help in time of trouble." Like many in our day, he had his Scriptures as well as his moral values confused.[11]

Another place you can find an abundance of lies is on TV, especially commercials. For example, "Feeling bad, just take this and you will be feeling great in minutes." "Do you want to lose weight? It is easy. All you have to do is buy ..." "Have you been injured in an accident? Then you need to call your friend attorney..."

You may be surprised, but some of the biggest lies that have ever been told are in the Bible. In the very first book of the Bible, we find the serpent lying to Eve.

> Now the serpent was more crafty than any of the wild animals the LORD God had made. He said to the woman, "Did God really say, 'You must not eat from any tree in the garden?' " The woman said to the serpent, "We may eat fruit from the trees in the garden, but God did say, 'You must not eat fruit from the tree that is in the middle of the garden, and you must not touch it, or you will die.' " "You will not certainly die," the serpent said to the woman (Genesis 3:1-4 NIV).

I assume the serpent had a forked tongue. If this were the case, Adam and Eve having been cast out of the garden, could have said, "He speaks with forked tongue – physically and figuratively." And all of God's children said, "Amen."

Jesus

Being lied to and being lied about have totally different effects on a person. For example, a person may tell you he went fishing all day yesterday and caught a ten pound bass.

But you know he was at home trying to fix his car. You were lied to but not lied about. On the other hand, if he had been telling people you were a swindler that would be something else. Being lied to can be as harmful as being lied about, but the latter has personal consequences concerning you.

[Jesus] said, "I am the way, the truth, and the life. No one comes to the Father except through Me" (John 14:6). Yet, Jesus, God incarnate has been lied about more than any other person that has ever lived. He (The Truth) has been lied about for thousands of years and will be lied about until His return.

During His earthly ministry, people were constantly lying about Him.

> But when the Pharisees heard it, they said: "This fellow doth not cast out devils, but by Beelzebub the prince of the devils" (Matthew 12:24 KJV).

Religious leaders searched for liars to convict Jesus.

> Inside, the leading priests and the entire high council were trying to find witnesses who would lie about Jesus, so they could put him to death. But even though they found many who agreed to give false witness, they could not use anyone's testimony. Finally, two men came forward (Matthew 26:59-60 NLT).

During Jesus' "trial," the high priest lied when he accused Jesus of blasphemy.

> But Jesus remained silent. Then the high priest said to him, "I demand in the name of the living God – tell us if you are the Messiah,

the Son of God." Jesus replied, "You have said it. And in the future you will see the Son of Man seated in the place of power at God's right hand—and coming on the clouds of heaven."

Then the high priest tore his clothing to show his horror and said, "Blasphemy! Why do we need other witnesses? You have all heard his blasphemy" (Matthew 26:63-65 NLT).

While on the cross, Jesus heard the lies about Himself.

The leading priests, the teachers of religious law, and the elders also mocked Jesus. "He saved others," they scoffed, "but he can't save himself! So he is the King of Israel, is he? Let him come down from the cross right now, and we will believe in him!" (Matthew 27:41-42 NLT).

Even after Jesus died and was buried, He was called a liar.

After sundown, the high priests and Pharisees arranged a meeting with Pilate. They said, "Sir, we just remembered that that liar announced while he was still alive, 'After three days I will be raised.' We've got to get that tomb sealed until the third day. There's a good chance his disciples will come and steal the corpse and then go around saying, 'He's risen from the dead.' Then we'll be worse off than before, the final deceit surpassing the first" (Matthew 27:62-64 MSG).

Liars and lies were determined to see Jesus crucified, and the good news He taught stopped. Jesus knew all about what was going on. He had previously pointed out the reason for their lies.

> Why do you not understand My speech? Because you are not able to listen to My word. You are of your father the devil, and the desires of your father you want to do. He was a murderer from the beginning, and does not stand in the truth, because there is no truth in him. When he speaks a lie, he speaks from his own resources, for he is a liar and the father of it. But because I tell the truth, you do not believe Me (John 8:43-45).

Notice Jesus said, "I tell you the truth." Furthermore, based on scripture, "Jesus Christ is the same yesterday, today, and forever" (Hebrews 13:8). Therefore, He is saying "I tell you the truth" to each of us today. Yet, like many people in the past, many people are rejecting The Truth [Jesus] in our time. Today some will say things like "God is dead" or "There are many gods" or "Jesus was only a prophet" or "Jesus is not God" and many will believe these lies. Nevertheless, The Truth [Jesus Christ] said,

> But when the Son of Man comes in his glory, and all the angels with him, then he will sit upon his glorious throne. All the nations will be gathered in his presence, and he will separate the people as a shepherd separates the sheep from the goats (Matthew 25:31-32 NLT).

You

Forked Tongue, Jesus and You. The "forked tongue" is still around today. It is present in every area of society. Some of the statements about Jesus in the previous verses are true and some are false. For example, the chief priests and the Pharisees called Jesus a liar (Matthew 27:63). Jesus not only said, "I tell you the truth" (John 8:45), but He said, "I am the truth" (John 14:6). Both of these statements cannot be true. A person must believe one or the other.

Personally, I believe Jesus. He is "the Truth." Concerning Satan, I believe what Jesus said about him, "He is a liar and the father of [lies]" (John 8:44b).

The facts demand a decision. "No man can serve two masters: for either he will hate the one, and love the other; or else he will hold to the one, and despise the other" (Matthew 6:24a KJV). "But if you refuse to serve the Lord, then choose today whom you will serve" (Joshua 24:15a NLT). But if you do believe Jesus is "the way, the truth and the life" (John 14:6a), then you will obey Him and have the assurance "that whoever believes in Him should not perish but have eternal life" (John 3:15). You have to decide who is speaking with a forked tongue. You cannot be neutral in this eternal matter. The decision is yours.

Chapter 15: Junk, Jesus and You

"One man's junk is another man's treasure."

Junk

As a boy raised in the country, my friends and I would often make many of the things we played with. We had an advantage because my dad was a mechanic. His shop, which he worked in after his 'day' job, was about fifty yards from our house. Some of the junk that was discarded from a repair job or from a wrecked auto was free to make many of the things we enjoyed.

While waiting our turn to play horseshoes, we would place the seats from a car on the ground against the wall of the shop. They made excellent seats to watch and wait. I know because the winners would keep on playing and the losers would have to let someone else play. My brother Jackie and his best friend Donald seemed to never lose, so I am an expert witness to the comfort of those seats. We often used junk to improve and replace other materials that we had. For instance, just about everybody had cardboard clipped to the forks of their bicycle to create a popping sound as it hit the spokes of the wheel. But a piece of gasket material would make a much louder sound and put the cardboard paper to shame.

Some of our junk projects took more thought and work than putting gasket material on a bicycle. Our wagons, for instance, were homemade from whatever material we could find. They were not made to pull around. They were made to ride. The county road that passed in front of our house had very little traffic and was basically level in front of our house and my dad's shop, but it went up a hill after you passed the house. The hill was perfect for our wagons. We tried all types of materials to make the wagons. We used iron wheels, solid rubber tires and air inflated tires. Our axles, tires, wheels, rope, seats, bolts, and nails may all be different, but one thing all our wagons had in common was that none had brakes. Once you pushed off at the top of the hill you were committed to the ride. On rare occasions, snow on the hill and an old hood from a truck would provide one of the most thrilling rides in the world. With three or four boys riding in the hood, every ride was different. Some rides were faster than others and some took different paths, but every time the end of the ride was unique.

Once we constructed a cable ride. Our group of boys got a piece of cable that had been thrown away, probably from an old pulp wood truck. Our swimming hole on Kelly Creek had a good swing so the cable wasn't needed there, but there was something else we could do with the cable. We could construct a new ride. First, we located the perfect place to construct our new ride. The place was a hollow. For those that don't know what a hollow is – think of a small valley. Then we put the cable through a piece of pipe large enough to slide easily up and down the cable. Next, we tied and nailed one end of the cable to a tree on one side of the hollow and tied and nailed the other end of the cable to a tree on the other side of the hollow. The first tree was higher in elevation than the second tree, but the second tree was higher than the lowest point of the ride. In other words, the cable was not pulled tight. It swagged toward the end. This caused the pipe to slow down and let us jump off at the end of the "ride." A small rope attached to the pipe allowed us to slide the pipe back to the starting point where axle grease, which was plentiful at my dad's shop, was applied to the front of the pipe to keep the ride running smoothly and coolly.

There was always junk around, and we always had plans to use what we had. Some plans worked out great and some failed, but we had a great time. I must admit, it would have been nice to have had a real swimming pool, but the creek and the swing on the tree were good enough for us. A store bought wagon certainly would have been much more appealing, but they didn't have the rope and the foot steering features of our wagons. The comparisons could go on. There are advantages to both – the country and the city. We were too busy to complain about what we didn't have, we just enjoyed all the wonderful junk that we did have. We used common everyday things that we had. Thank God for junk.

Using what you have is nothing new; many people have done this throughout history. The following are just a few examples found in the Bible:

In the book of Judges, we find the children of Israel had been in bondage for twenty years to "Jabin king of Canaan, that reigned in Hazor; the captain of whose host was Sisera, which dwelt in Harosheth of the Gentiles" (Judges 4:2 KJV). At that time Deborah, a prophetess and judge, summoned Barak to assume military leadership of the Israelites and to defeat the Canaanites under the command of Sisera. Barak would not go unless Deborah went with him: "If you go with me, I will go; but if you don't go with me, I won't go" (Judges

4:8 NIV). Sounds like some of the men in the church today. Anyway, Deborah does go with Barak, and the children of Israel defeat the Canaanites, but Sisera the leader of the Canaanites escaped to the Kenites where he thought he would be safe.

> Sisera, meanwhile, fled on foot to the tent of Jael, the wife of Heber the Kenite, because there was an alliance between Jabin king of Hazor and the family of Heber the Kenite. Jael went out to meet Sisera and said to him, "Come, my lord, come right in. Don't be afraid." So he entered her tent, and she covered him with a blanket.
>
> "I'm thirsty," he said. "Please give me some water." She opened a skin of milk, gave him a drink, and covered him up. "Stand in the doorway of the tent," he told her. "If someone comes by and asks you, 'Is anyone in there?' say 'No.' "
>
> But Jael, Heber's wife, picked up a tent peg and a hammer and went quietly to him while he lay fast asleep, exhausted. She drove the peg through his temple into the ground, and he died (Judges 4:17-21 NIV).

An Israelite should have killed Sisera in battle. Instead, Jael, a Kenite woman, used milk, a tent peg and a hammer to kill the commander of the Cananite army. She used what she had.

In the book of Genesis, we find Noah using what was available to him to build the ark. "Make yourself an ark of gopher wood; make rooms in the ark, and cover it inside and outside with pitch" (Genesis 6:14).

In Jeremiah 13, Jeremiah didn't use a Power Point presentation nor did he have hand-out notes to foretell what would happen to Judah and Jerusalem. Instead he used a linen girdle to demonstrate how the people had become "ruined and completely useless" (Jeremiah 13:7).

In Acts 16, Lydia didn't ask God to do a miracle to provide for the young church. She was a businesswoman and used her income to support the church. She used what was available to her.

In Acts 8, as an Ethiopian eunuch who had "great authority under Candace the queen of the Ethiopians, who had the charge of all her treasure" (Acts 8:27) was returning to Ethiopia. Philip led him to become a believer. As a result, the Ethiopian wanted to be baptized, but he didn't wait until he returned to the palaces of the queen. Instead, "as they traveled along the road, they came to some water and the eunuch said, 'Look, here is water. What can stand in the way of my being baptized?' " (Acts 8:36 NIV). We are not given any detail concerning the water. It really doesn't matter whether it was a stream, a pool of water or whatever. They used what they had available to them.

In Judges 15, Samson used a jaw bone of a donkey to kill a thousand of his enemies, the Philistines. "He [Samson] found a fresh jawbone of a donkey, reached out his hand and took it, and killed a thousand men with it" (Judges 15:15). Samson didn't have a sword, but he used what was available.

In Joshua 2, Rahab used stalks of flax to save the lives of the two spies who had been sent to Jericho to check out the city.

> The king of Jericho sent word to Rahab: "Bring out the men who came to you to stay the night in your house. They're spies; they've come to spy out the whole country." The woman had

taken the two men and hidden them. She said, "Yes, two men did come to me, but I didn't know where they'd come from" (Joshua 2:3-4 MSG).

After the king's men left and the spies were safe "she let them down by a rope through the window" (Joshua 2:15a NIV). Rahab used what was available and saved the spies.

Yet, one of the greatest examples of people using what is available to them is found in Acts 12.

That's when King Herod got it into his head to go after some of the church members. He murdered James, John's brother. When he saw how much it raised his popularity ratings with the Jews, he arrested Peter – all this during Passover Week, mind you – and had him thrown in jail, putting four squads of four soldiers each to guard him. He was planning a public lynching after Passover. All the time that Peter was under heavy guard in the jailhouse, the church prayed for him most strenuously. Then the time came for Herod to bring him out for the kill. That night, even though shackled to two soldiers, one on either side, Peter slept like a baby. And there were guards at the door keeping their eyes on the place. Herod was taking no chances!

Suddenly there was an angel at his side and light flooding the room. The angel shook Peter and got him up: "Hurry!" The handcuffs fell off his wrists. The angel said, "Get dressed. Put on your shoes." Peter did it. Then, "Grab your coat and let's get out of here." Peter followed him, but didn't believe it was really an angel – he thought he was dreaming. Past the first guard and then the second, they came to the iron gate that led into the city. It swung open before them on its own, and they were out on the street, free as the breeze. At the first intersection the angel left him, going his own way. That's when Peter realized it was no dream. "I can't believe it – this really happened! The Master sent his angel and rescued me from Herod's vicious little production and the spectacle the Jewish mob was looking forward to" (Acts 12:1-11 MSG).

Peter was not rescued by an army that overpowered Herod's guards. Peter was rescued by the prayers of the church. Notice in the scripture above that "All the time that Peter was under heavy guard in the jailhouse, the church prayed for him most strenuously" (Acts 12:5 MSG). The church used what was available to them – prayer.

Jesus

Jesus, God incarnate, used what was available to Him. On one occasion Jesus could have used a good sound system to speak to a great crowd of people, but He didn't have one. You may say, "They didn't have sound systems at that time." That would be a true statement, but Jesus was and is and always will be God the Son and a sound system would have been no problem to the Creator. He could have "floated" up in the air so that the great multitude could see and hear Him. He chose not to do that or any other miracle in order for the multitude to hear him. Instead, He used what He had available. Notice what Matthew says about the incident:

> On the same day Jesus went out of the house and sat by the sea. And great multitudes were gathered together to Him, so that He got into a boat and sat; and the whole multitude stood on the shore (Matthew 13:1-2).

The boat was an ideal pulpit to speak from. The water was a natural sound system. The shore provided plenty of seating. As a result, Jesus had taken what was available to Him and created an outdoor sanctuary.

John tells of another occasion where Jesus used what was available to Him to restore the sight of a blind man.

> When He had said these things, He spat on the ground and made clay with the saliva; and He anointed the eyes of the blind man with the clay (John 9:6).

He didn't wrap the man's eyes with fine purple cloth or use some type of ointment. He used what was available. He used mud. When the scribes and Pharisees brought a woman caught in the very act of adultery to Jesus, Jesus wrote in the sand. We don't know what He wrote, but the scribes and Pharisees "being convicted by their own conscience went out one by one" (John 8:9a). He didn't have a dry erase board; instead, He used what was available to Him – sand.

You

Junk, Jesus and You. Growing up, I certainly had a lot of junk available to me. My friends and I used all that we could and it brought great joy into our lives. In the Bible, we see individuals and Jesus using what was available to them in their

146

everyday lives.

What about you? Are you standing around saying, "If only I had..." Look around! You *do* have available all that you need to accomplish God's mission. You are uniquely made to use what God has placed in your life. If you have a lawnmower, you can cut grass for an elderly person. If you can cook, you can prepare a meal for someone that is homebound. If you have a computer or phone, you can encourage someone. If you own a car, you can provide transportation for someone. The list could go on and on. If you can't see what is available to you, ask God to show you. Let me remind you, there is one thing that is available to all of us – prayer.

May you use whatever God has placed in your life in order to give God glory and may you start today.

Chapter 16: Electronics, Jesus and You

"Our technology may have exceeded our understanding."[1]

Electronics

Growing up as a mechanic's son helped me understand how mechanical things worked. However, when it comes to electronics, I have no idea how a lot of them work. I have a friend Steve who can explain the way things work and tell you the meaning of amplitude, analog, digital, bandwidth, capacitor, distortion, frequency, inductor, resistor, wavelength and probably a hundred more terms – words that I had to look up just to make reference to. He works with electronics every day, but he cannot explain electronics simply enough for me to understand. Why? It is electronics! Let me share my difficulty.

I understand how you can take two soup cans and a string and make a telephone. Simply punch a hole in the middle of the cans, put a string through the holes and tie a knot in both ends of the string. Next, stretch the string tight from one can to the other to allow the sound waves to travel across the string. After that, one person can talk into one can and the other person can hear what the first person said. If 'reception' is poor, just shorten the string.

However, when it comes to electronic phones, I have no idea how they work. For instance, when I use my land line phone, I pick up the handset, push some numbers and hear a ringing sound. The person answers another phone at the other end and the conversation begins. I don't understand how my conversation can travel over wires for thousands of miles and not get mixed up with the millions of other conversations that are using the same wires.

The cell phone is more difficult to understand. When I use my cell phone, I am talking into a small plastic object that is filled with electronic stuff with no strings or wires attached. My words take to the air and are received by another plastic object filled with electronic stuff. My conversation may be with someone hundreds of miles away. I realize our conversation is not the only one taking place. There may be billions of cell phone conversations and billions of people texting, twittering, and whatever else can be done, all at the same time. In addition, AM, FM, short wave and ham radio around the world add more words and music to the air. TV stations not only add words, but they fill the air with black and white, color and 3-D pictures. Plus, I cannot fathom the amount of communication the internet is launching into the air at the same time.

Electronic words, music and pictures are not the only things filling the air. It would be impossible to guess the number of transactions that are in the air when people use their credit cards to purchase everything from gas to clothing to groceries, etc. Even TV remotes fill the air with signals when we point these small plastic objects filled with electronic stuff at the TV to change it to another program, control the volume, record a program, and much more. In addition, many people have sound systems, home security systems, heating and air conditioners, lamps, etc. that can be controlled by a remote electronic device. Most vehicles are full of electronics that can be controlled by remote. You can lock, unlock and start your car and not be near it. Just push some buttons and the command goes through the air and the car obeys.

These are just a few of the electronic devices an ordinary family may use. Besides these everyday gadgets, I am amazed to hear and see some of the electronic devices in the medical field, in the military or used by NASA. It is inconceivable to think of all the electronic things in the air.

Now with all those pictures, words, music, electronic commands and other "electronic things" just soaring through the air, how does my simple phone conversation with my friend get through all the mess? It seems to me there should be a massive electronic traffic jam in the air!

I don't understand how all of these electronic inventions work, but there is something that I must admit. I may not understand how they work, but I use them and trust them with some major areas of my life.

Jesus

In a way, Jesus and electronics have something in common. Take a television, for example. When I go to purchase a TV, the employee at the store may show me one on display and tell me all about the TV. I trust what he is saying and purchase the TV, carry it home, plug it in, follow the instructions and enjoy it. I don't understand how it works, but it does.

Before I became a Christian, I had many people tell me about Jesus. People like my mom, Sunday school teachers, preachers, and many more. I read the Bible and thought about what I heard and read. The Holy Spirit convicted me that I was a sinner. As a result, by grace I was saved, through faith. But, unlike the purchase of the television, I didn't purchase my salvation. It was a gift. I received the gift of salvation and have been enjoying it ever since. Even though I took possession of the TV and took possession of the gift of salvation, I still don't understand all about the TV and my little finite mind certainly cannot comprehend Almighty God.

When I received the television, I also received an instruction book with it. I must confess, I have not studied it like I should. I know enough about the TV to see what I want to see. I am sure there are a lot more features that I don't use, but I watch TV very little and frankly don't care about knowing every feature. With the quality of television's today, if I did study and learn all the extra features, the TV would quit working and I would have to purchase a new one with new instructions.

This is not the same when it comes to salvation. When I accepted the gift of salvation, I already had my instruction book. It is the Bible. Unlike the TV instruction book, the Holy Spirit placed a desire in me to read the Bible, so I can enjoy what God has given me. In addition, God's Word has not changed and never will.

Henrietta C. Mears in her book, *What the Bible Is All About*, makes the following simple yet profound statement: "The Bible is God's written revelation of His will to men. Its central theme is salvation through Jesus Christ."[2] I agree with her totally. The Bible does not try to prove the existence of God or a number of theological issues that man seems to be so intent on understanding. He is God; we are His creation, not His equal. The prophet Isaiah confirmed this when he wrote:

"My thoughts are nothing like your thoughts," says the LORD. "And my ways are far beyond anything you could imagine. For just as the heavens are higher than the earth, so my ways are higher than your ways and my thoughts higher than your thoughts" (Isaiah 55:8-9 NLT).

We cannot understand God, but "Man's chief end is to glorify God, and enjoy Him forever."[3]

Now before I continue, let me repeat what I said earlier. There are a lot of people like my friend Steve who understand all about electronics. Steve will tell you that he does not understand all about Almighty God. As a matter of fact, if anyone told me they did understand everything about God, it would confirm to me that they know very little about Him.

Furthermore, there have been and are many who claim to be god. But the question is not about others. The question is, "Can we trust Jesus Christ?" Notice, I did not say, "Do you understand Jesus Christ?" "Is He the Son of God?" "Is He God the Son?" "Is He God?" I believe He is who He says He is. Jesus is God incarnate. I don't understand everything about Jesus, but I believe/trust Him.

This "not understanding God" certainly didn't start with me. During Jesus' ministry, there were many that trusted/believed in Him even though they did not understand. For example, in John 11, we find the story of Jesus raising Lazarus from the dead. Lazarus was the brother of Martha and "Mary which anointed the Lord with ointment, and wiped his feet with her hair" (John 11:2 KJV). But the focus is not about a person being in a tomb for four days and being brought back to life. Let me explain: Martha makes a confession of faith that Jesus is "the Christ, the Son of God" (John 11:27). Mary makes it clear that Jesus could have prevented Lazarus' death if only He had been there (John 11:32). Both statements show faith in Jesus, but when Jesus instructs them to take away the stone from the tomb, Martha has reservations about this, when she says: "by this time there is a stench, for he has been dead four days" (John 11:39). In other words, she could not understand why Jesus wanted the stone rolled away. "Jesus said to her, 'Did I not say to you that if you would believe you would see the glory of God?' " (John 11:40). She did not respond by saying, "Lord, I don't understand why you want us to do this." Instead, "they took away the stone" (John 11:41).

Whether we had lived during Jesus' earthly ministry or today, understanding all about Jesus is not something that can be comprehended by the human mind. For example, the divinity of Jesus is presented throughout the Bible by others and by Jesus himself.

Joseph is explicitly told of Jesus' divinity by an angel when the angel told him:

> She [Mary] will bring forth a Son, and you shall call His name JESUS, for He will save His people from their sins…and they shall call His name Immanuel, which is translated, "God with us" (Matthew1:21,23b).

John confirmed the angel's proclamation of "God with us" when he wrote "The Word was God" and "the Word was made flesh and dwelt among us" (John1:1,14 KJV).

> Peter said, "We have come to believe and know that You are that Christ, the Son of the living God" (John 6:69).
> The disciples worshipped Him, saying, "Truly You are the Son of God " (Matthew14:33).
> A Roman solider acknowledged, "Truly this Man was the Son of God!" (Mark 15:39b).

154

Notice in the above verses the words "believe," "of a truth," and "acknowledged" are used, but none of those statements use the word "understand." There are many more individuals in the Bible that acknowledged Jesus as God, but like the above, they do not use the word "understand."

Now, let's look at some of the statements Jesus said about Himself concerning his deity:

> Jesus said, "I and My Father are one" (John 10:30).
>
> "For I have come down from heaven, not to do My own will, but the will of Him who sent Me" (John 6:38).
>
> "I who speak to you am He [the Messiah]" (John 4:26).
>
> Since only God can forgive sins, Jesus is affirming His deity when he said, "Son, thy sins are forgiven you" (Mark 2:56).
>
> "Also I say unto you, whosoever shall confess Me before men, him the Son of Man also will confess before the angels of God. But he who denies Me before men will be denied before the angels of God" (Luke 12:8-9).
>
> But Jesus kept silent. And the high priest answered and said to Him, "I put You under oath by the living God; Tell us if You are the Christ, the Son of God!" Jesus said to him, "It is as you said" (Matthew 26:63-64a).
>
> Jesus said to them, "Most assuredly, I say to you, before Abraham was, I AM" (John 8:58).

In the few verses above, the divinity of Jesus is acknowledged and confirmed by Jesus himself. Also, notice what Jesus said to Nicodemus:

> For God so loved the world that He gave His only begotten Son, that whoever believes in Him should not perish but have everlasting life. For God did not send His Son into the world to condemn the world, but that the world through Him might be saved. He who believes in Him is not condemned; but he who does not believe is condemned already, because he has not believed in the name of the only begotten Son of God (John 3:16-18).

Because Jesus is the Son of God, our belief in Him is necessary to have everlasting life and not be condemned. Notice that nowhere does Jesus say you must understand Him. The word "understand" is not to be found.

You may be thinking that other religions have holy books and leaders too. All I have referenced is the Bible and Jesus. That is true, but Jesus is the only one to proclaim the gospel of His death, burial and resurrection. Not only did He proclaim it, He did die, was buried and rose from the grave. If nothing else convinces you that Jesus is who He said He is, the resurrection should. I find no eye-witnesses of other spiritual leaders being seen after their death. Yet, Scripture tells us

> ...that he was buried, and that He rose again the third day according to Scriptures and that He was seen by Cephas, then by the twelve. After that He was seen by over five hundred brethren at once, of whom the greater part remain to the present, but some have fallen asleep. After that

He was seen by James, then by all the apostles
(I Corinthians 15:4-7).

Furthermore, Jesus gave additional evidence of His divinity when He spoke to his disciples concerning what He would be doing after His ascension. "I go to prepare a place for you. And if I go and prepare a place for you, I will come again, and receive you to myself; that where I am, there you may be also" (John 14:2b-3). In this same chapter, Jesus declared the only way to go to the place He would prepare for them was Him.

> And where I go you know, and the way you know. Thomas said to Him, "Lord, we do not know where You are going, and how can we know the way?" Jesus said to him, "I am the way, the truth, and the life. No one comes to the Father, except through Me" (John 14:4-6).

These verses state that the only way to heaven and to the Father is Jesus. Any other way will not get you there. Good works, false religions, whatever, will not allow you to come to the Father. "Jesus' exclusive claim is unmistakable. It forces an unconditional response. Jesus invites people to accept or reject him, making it clear that partial acceptance is rejection. His self-description invalidates alternative plans of salvation."[4] All of this is a matter of faith, but it is not a matter of understanding.

The gospel is simple, but if anyone doesn't want to believe the gospel there are thousands of excuses not to believe. One of those excuses is "I don't understand." Yet at the same time, you don't understand a lot of modern technology, but you accept that.

Faith in Jesus Christ is not mentally understanding Him. As I said before, it is impossible to understand God. "For my thoughts are not your thoughts, nor are your ways My ways," says the Lord (Isaiah 55:8). Faith is not feelings or emotions. Faith is confidence that is based on the fact that "there is one God, and one Mediator between God and men, the Man Christ Jesus, who gave Himself a ransom for all" (I Timothy 2:5-6a). Dr. J. Vernon McGee (*Thru the Bible Radio Network*) helps us to recognize this fact when he wrote:

> It is not the amount of knowledge you have, but the kind of knowledge that is important. It is whom you know. Do you know Jesus Christ? In the same way, it is not the amount of faith you have but the kind of faith that is important...It is Christ who saves. One can believe in the wrong thing. It is the object of faith which is so important...The gospel is that Jesus died for our sins, was buried, and rose again. Those are the facts. Our knowledge of the facts and our response to that knowledge is faith. Faith is trusting Christ as our own Savior.[5]

You

Allow me to say this one more time: I do not understand electronics and my little finite mind cannot begin to comprehend Almighty God. There are a number of questions for which I have no answers. For example, if space ends, what is beyond space? Where did God come from? If the universe began with a bang, where did the elements for the bang come from? If evolution is true and you keep on going back in the process, do you not finally get to a place where there was nothing and then there was something? If something comes from nothing is that not creation? To have creation, do you not have to have a creator?

Just from those few questions, it is apparent I don't understand a lot of things. However, what I do understand is that at one time in my life, I realized I was a sinner. As a sinner, I was separated from God (Isaiah 59:2a) and knew those who do not know God would experience everlasting punishment and separation from God (2 Thessalonians 1:8b-9). Then I believed God sent His Son to die on the cross for my sins. I believed Jesus is the only way to receive forgiveness and have eternal life. I confessed with my mouth the Lord Jesus and I believed in my heart that God had raised Him from the dead and I was saved (Romans 10:9).

Electronics, Jesus and You. Everyone must decide to believe Jesus or not. This chapter was simply to share the good news that you do not have to understand everything about Jesus to become a Christian. I realize the Bible has the answers, but to be honest, I don't understand everything in the Bible. It is comforting to know others have had the same problem. For example, one person said:

> One moonlit night in the mountains of California I went out alone with my Bible. I laid my open Bible on the stump of a tree and prayed, "O Lord, I don't understand everything in this Book, but I accept it by faith as the Word of the living God." Since that moment I've never doubted that the Bible is the Word of God. God has confirmed this to me, as I have witnessed the power of the Word of God at work in the lives of people.[6]

The man that said that became the greatest evangelist of our time, Dr. Billy Graham.

You may be refusing to take a step of faith and believe because you don't understand. If I refused to enjoy the benefits of what I don't understand, I wouldn't be using any electronic devices. Even worse, if I refused to enjoy the benefits of what God has provided, just because I don't understand everything about God, I would spend eternity in hell. I may not understand, but I believe/have faith in my Savior. Jesus is the object of my faith, not my understanding. Even though Dr. Graham was honest about his not understanding everything in God's Word, God has used him in a mighty way. I pray you will be honest about your understanding of God and go to Him just as you are.

Chapter 17: Parents, Jesus and You

"Parents wonder why the streams are bitter, when they themselves have poisoned the fountain."[1]

Parents

One thing that all of us have in common is parents. We all had or have a mom and dad. Parents can be sorry, low down selfish and self-absorbed, ignoring their children. Or parents can be loving, unselfish, sacrificial and want only the best for their child. As I have mentioned before, just because a woman can give birth to a baby, does not make that woman a mother. Likewise, there is a great difference between a father that loves his child and a person that has the title of "father" but in reality is nothing but a sperm donor.

As children, we didn't have a choice of who our biological father and mother would be. As a pastor, I have talked with individuals that despised their mother or father. I have also seen others who dearly loved their parents. I have conducted funerals where the children could not seem to say enough about being blessed with their mother or father. Sadly, I have seen a parent lie on their death bed for weeks and their adult child never comes to visit. Even though they professed to be mature Christians, their hearts had grown hard and cold toward their parent.

I have visited in the home of what seemed to be a very loving family. The mother, the father, and the son had all made professions of faith. As an only child, the young man seemed to have had everything. Nevertheless, his combination of anger and alcohol resulted in him murdering his mother and his father. Now, visits are not made to the home of the family but to the cemetery or prison.

I could continue to give more personal examples of relationships between children and parents. Some were good and some were bad. The good relationships usually produced praise and honor and the bad relationships usually produced cursing and dishonor. However, the relationship between a parent and a child does not automatically determine what kind of person the child will become. Ungodly parents don't always have ungodly children, and godly parents don't always have godly children.

Dr. Herschel H. Hobbs, a leading Southern Baptist theologian, made the following observation concerning parents.

> Through the years I have counseled with godly parents whose children did not turn out to be all they and the Lord wanted them to be. Invariably the parents asked, "Where did we fail in rearing our child?" All the while I knew they had done all that parents could do to rear the child in the fear and admonition of the Lord.
>
> My reply was always as follows:
>
> You did your best. But there comes a time when they encounter influences contrary to your teaching. We have our children for

such a short time. All that we can do is teach them the will and way of the Lord, lead them to have faith in Him, and instill in them principles of righteous living that will strengthen and guide them in the choices they must make. And then pray for them. Both parents and children must be willing to follow God's guidance.²

Each person must take responsibility for the choices they make. The following verses found in the Old and New Testaments confirm this. Ezekiel writes, "The person who sins is the one who will die. The child will not be punished for the parent's sins, and the parent will not be punished for the child's sins. Righteous people will be rewarded for their own righteous behavior, and wicked people will be punished for their own wickedness" (Ezekiel 18:20 NLT). The apostle Paul wrote: "For we are each responsible for our own conduct" (Galatians 6:5 NLT). "So then every one of us shall give account of himself to God" (Romans 14:12). As a parent, you cannot make your child a saint or a sinner.

Not only is the principle of individual accountability of a parent and a child set forth in Scripture, it is confirmed with various examples throughout the Bible. For example, in the second chapter of Joshua, we are told how Rahab, a prostitute in Jericho, saved the lives of the two Israelite spies. In return, Rahab, her father, mother, brothers, sisters, and all that they had were not harmed when Jericho was destroyed. Scripture does not give us details concerning how Rahab and her family were assimilated in with the Israelites, but I am confident Rahab was looked down on by some. I based this statement not on Scripture, but on human beings being human beings. Nevertheless, Rahab became the wife of Salmon, an Israelite, and she gave birth to Boaz (Matthew 1:5). Boaz could have been made fun of or looked down on because his mother was a Gentile and had been a prostitute. We don't know. We do know that Boaz became a "mighty man of wealth" (Ruth 2:1), respected (Ruth 2:4), and compassionate (Ruth 2:9). He was kindhearted and wanted to help the less fortunate (Ruth 2:11). In the genealogy of Jesus found in the first chapter of Matthew, we find that this son of a prostitute becomes the great grandfather of King David.

Josiah is another example of individual accountability. Josiah's grandfather was Manasseh and "He sacrificed his own son in the fire, practiced divination, sought omens, and consulted mediums and spirits. He did much evil in the eyes of the LORD, arousing his anger" (II Kings 21:6 NIV). Josiah was the son of King Amon (II Kings 2:24).

> He [Amon] did that which was evil in the sight of the LORD, as his father Manasseh did. And he walked in all the way that his father walked in, and served the idols that his father served, and worshipped them: And he forsook the LORD God of his fathers, and walked not in the way of the LORD (II Kings 21:20-22 KJV).

If ever there were two evil male influences on a person, it was the influence Manasseh and Amon had on Josiah. Josiah could have followed the example of his father and grandfather and become an evil king. Instead, Josiah became Judah's greatest king. "Neither before nor after Josiah was there a king like him who turned to the LORD as he did – with all his heart and with all his soul and with all his strength, in accordance with all the Law of Moses" (II Kings 23:25 NIV). But when Josiah died, his son Jehoahaz began to reign, and "he did that which was evil in the sight of the Lord" (II Kings 23:32a KJV). Here we have an ungodly father (Amon) whose son

164

Josiah becomes the most godly king of Judah. Then there is Jehoahaz, the son of Josiah, that does "Evil in the sight of the Lord" (II Kings 23:32).

There are many more examples in the Bible. Jehoshaphat, a godly king, did "that which was right in the eyes of the Lord" (I Kings 22:43 KJV). His son, Jehoram, was an ungodly king for "he did evil in the sight of the LORD" (II Chronicles 21:5-6). Jotham, a good king, who "did what was right in the sight of the Lord" (II Chronicles 27:2) had a son, Ahaz, who was an evil king and "he did not do what was right in the sight of the LORD" (II Chronicles 28:1). Ahaz had a son, Hezekiah, who was a godly king, "who did that which was right in the sight of the Lord" (II Chronicles 29:2 KJV).

Examples of godly parents having ungodly children and ungodly parents having godly parents are not just found in the Bible. You probably know some yourself. You can find examples in the churches, schools and companies throughout your area. The examples don't discriminate by age, physical ability, religion, race, gender, wealth, power, or any other category. They may be men or women that you know who were raised by good Christian parents but later became criminals. On the other hand, you may know men and women that are respected and loved but had terrible parents. They didn't allow what their parents were to determine what they became. As a result, they have become role models and an inspiration to all who did not have godly parents. Just like Josiah and Hezekiah, they are "Bibles" that people can see and living testimonies that a child does not have to become like their parents.

Jesus

We know at least one parent was at Calvary – Mary. Some of Jesus' last words were spoken to John asking him to take care of her (John19:26-27). We read nothing about Joseph, but in all probability, Joseph had died. I say this because Joseph was a just and kind man (Matthew 1:19). I believe if he had been alive, he would have been at Calvary and Jesus would not have asked John to take care of Mary. What about the parents of the two thieves? Were their fathers there? Were their mothers there? We don't know. If they were there, did the thieves hear, "I love you son?" If their parents were there, we know one set of parents heard their son say to Jesus, "Aren't you the Messiah? Save yourself and us!" (Luke 23:39 NIV). Meanwhile, the other parents heard their son say:

> "Don't you fear God," he said, "since you are under the same sentence? We are punished justly, for we are getting what our deeds deserve. But this man has done nothing wrong." Then he said, "Jesus, remember me when you come into your kingdom." Jesus answered him, "Truly I tell you, today you will be with me in paradise" (Luke 23:40-43 NIV).

Both men crucified with Jesus were criminals. Their parents could have been evil or godly. But one criminal changed. He may have wasted his life up to that point, but he did change on his cross. We don't know, but just maybe the parents heard the promise that Jesus had made to him. If they did, then three days later they probably heard: "He [Jesus] is risen. He is alive." One mother and father would have had hope and may have become Christians. One mother and father would remember their son cursing Jesus. Maybe both sets of parents heard a promise and believed. Maybe they repented. Maybe they changed. Maybe they didn't.

You

Parents, Jesus and You. You may be saying, "You don't know what the parents did or didn't do," and that would be true. What I do know is that one thief took responsibility for what he had done. Normally, this is not the case. As Lewis Laws, who was America's most famous warden once stated, "Few of the criminals in Sing Sing [Prison] regard themselves as bad men."[3] But one thief did see himself as bad and didn't blame others for his predicament. His past didn't matter. The criminal may have had a criminal record as long as his arm but that did not keep him from changing. His attitude, his mindset, and his faith all changed on a cross. The thief was the only one that could have made the change. No one else could make the decision for him. As a result, he was forgiven and is with Jesus today.

If you have never asked Jesus to forgive you, notice the sequence of events at Calvary. First, the criminal acknowledged himself as a sinner and expressed faith in Jesus. Jesus is willing to forgive you just as he did the criminal on the cross. It doesn't matter if your parents were mean, hateful, evil and abusive parents; you don't have to be like them. They have to answer to God for what they have done. If your past, your friends, your parents, or anything else is keeping you from changing, then they are controlling your life.

If you died today, would you be with Jesus? It is not too late to change. Don't let anything keep you from a personal relationship with Jesus. What is done is done. Don't allow the past to destroy your future. He is waiting to accept you just as you are. Then you can be "certain that God, who began the good work within you, will continue his work until it is finally finished on the day when Christ Jesus returns" (Philippians 1:6 NLT).

Let's not forget, change is not just for the unbeliever. As a Christian, if we are guilty of making excuses by pointing to the past, then we are living a defeated life. It is time to change. God has plans for all believers, "plans to prosper you and not to harm you, plans to give you hope and a future" (Jeremiah 29:11 NIV).

Chapter 18: Accounting, Jesus and You

"So then each of us shall give account of himself to God." (Romans 14:12)

WARNING!

Before you read this chapter, I must warn you of something.

I asked a person to read this chapter and give me their honest opinion of it. They suggested that the chapter could be left out because to some it would be hard to follow the flow of the business example. They added, "You have been in the business world all of your adult life. You understand all those accounting terms, but a lot of people don't."

I must admit this is not my customary "Jesus and You" chapter. However, contrary to the advice that I received, I have decided to include this chapter for those that will understand it, especially for all the honest, hardworking men and women in business. Out of envy, some get criticized as greedy because they are successful. Yet, many preach the gospel everyday by the way they conduct themselves in business. Saint Francis of Assisi is often quoted as saying, "Preach the Gospel at all times and when necessary use words." Whether or not he said this is debated, but the fact that many working men and women live this quote cannot be debated. Not only are they examples, they do use words when the Holy Spirit has gone before them and prepared a person's heart to hear the Word. They understand what "the bottom line" means – in business and in life. They understand fulfillment in life is not found in wealth, power, and fame but in a personal relationship with God. If no one else understands this chapter, I hope those people mentioned above will enjoy the similarity of earthly accounting and heavenly accounting.

Then again, I believe more than the people I have mentioned above will enjoy it. Hopefully, you will. But if you are the kind of person that finds it hard to follow the flow of the business example, please accept my apology and go to the next chapter. It contains some personal thoughts that I believe you will relate to.

Accounting, Jesus and You

Accounting

The word "accounting" can bring to mind a lot of different things to different people. To a college student, it may be a required course to get a degree. Accounting could bring thoughts of the IRS and of an audit. The word "accounting" could make a person think of companies that used fraudulent accounting methods to cheat people of their life savings. Accounting may cause thoughts of bank statements, balancing the check book, budgets and thousands of other good and bad things. To others, accounting may bring thoughts of an accountant sitting at a desk wearing a visor doing boring, boring work. Speaking of accountants, they are certainly not at the top of the "what I want to be when I grow up" list.

Before I go on I must confess, I am a "bean counter" and proud of it. After graduating from UAB with a degree in accounting, our livelihood was provided by accounting, so I am certainly not going to belittle the hand that fed us. Also, I want you to know that accounting is not such a boring occupation. You get to meet all kinds of people and actually see how a business works. I realize that for some accountants this may not be the case, but it was for me.

My first accounting job with a large company was in the fixed assets department. We were responsible for physically locating and placing property identification tags on equipment in different plants. This allowed me to meet many people at various positions in the company and see firsthand how different plants operate. Many of the people I met became great friends.

Another time, I was assigned to a team to audit a jewelry store. During the audit, one of the items I was to verify was a particular ring. According to the records, there were supposed to be a fairly large number of these rings. I could only find one and it was on display. It was a beautiful ring, displayed on a velvet cloth. Thinking the others would probably be in a vault, I asked the manager for the location of the other rings. He led me to a plain cabinet and pulled out a drawer and there, looking like a bunch of fish hooks tangled up in a tackle box, was the balance of the inventory. The ring on display looked so expensive. The ones in the drawer looked like something you would win at an arcade. Presentation made the difference.

I could go on, but accounting definitely has been good to me.

No matter what you think of accounting, it is basically a

language. It communicates what is going on in the business world, and just like any other language if you don't use it you lose it. I can testify to this fact. Over the years, I have used my accounting skills less and less, and as a result, I have forgotten much of what I once knew. Now I go to my CPA friends like Randy in Sumiton or Larry in Moody for advice. But I probably will never forget the importance of two financial statements. They are the "Income Statement" and the "Balance Sheet." These two statements may only be a single page per statement, but represent everything concerning a company.

The balance sheet shows the financial condition of a business on a particular date. For example, the financial condition of a business on December 31, 20XX. It is the financial condition for that day and that day only. The balance sheet will show what a business owns (Assets) and how the business got what it owns (Liabilities and Owner's Equity). The following is a simplified example.

ACME AUTO CLINIC BALANCE SHEET
December 31, 20XX

Assets	**Liabilities & Owner's Equity**
Cash.............$ 25,000	Liabilities: Loan......$150,000
Building........$175,000	Owners Equity...... $ 50,000
Total Assets **$200,000**	**Total Liabilities &** **$200,000** **Owner's Equity**

This is what the business has   This is how the business got it

In the above example, assets would be cash and a building. Liabilities and Owners Equity is how a business acquired the assets. In the above example, the assets were acquired by the owner putting in $50,000 of his money and getting a loan for the balance. Another way to help understand a balance sheet is to remember a simple equation:

$$\textbf{Assets} = \textbf{Liabilities} + \textbf{Owner's Equity}$$
$$\textbf{\$200,000} = \textbf{\$150,000} + \textbf{\$50,000}$$

In the above example, the business owned a total of $200,000 in assets. The company acquired the assets by liabilities (debt) and by the owner's equity (investment by the owner). The net worth of the company would be the assets less the liabilities of the company. For example, if you owned a company that had assets of $200,000 and liabilities (debt) of $150,000, the net worth or book value would be $50,000.

Now I want to change our discussion from companies to individuals. Every person has their own personal financial balance sheet. For example, when John Doe applies for a loan at a bank, the information that he provides will allow the bank to generate a balance sheet on him. It will tell the bank his net worth. John Doe's simplified balance sheet may be the following:

JOHN DOE BALANCE SHEET
Dec. 31, 20XX

Assets		Liabilities & Owner's Equity	
Home ....$ 275,000		Liabilities:	
Stocks, 401K, etc..$ 150,000			
Cash................$ 1,500		Home Mortgage...........$170,000	
Savings............. $ 7,000		Credit Cards.............$ 9,500	
Autos................$ 30,000		Student Loan............ ..$ 20,500	
Home Content...... $ 15,000		Auto Loans................$ 20,000	
Personal Items......$ 7,500		**Total Liabilities $220,000**	
		Owner's Equity......... $266,000	
Total Assets	**$486,000**	**Total Liabilities and... $486,000**	
		Owner's Equity	

173

In this case, John Doe's equity/net worth would be $266,000. In other words, if John Doe sold all his assets and received cash, he would have a total of $486,000 in cash. If he then paid his liabilities/debts with the cash, he would have $266,000 left that would be his.

The banker who is considering extending the loan to John Doe will not make his decision based on personality, looks, character, age, etc. The balance sheet will determine if John Doe is to receive the loan or not. With that in mind, let's move on to more important accounting principles.

Jesus

First, let me say that I thank God our worth to Him is not based on an earthly balance sheet. If it were, I would be in trouble. Our worth is not based on what we own. We own nothing. "For we brought nothing into this world, and it is certain we can carry nothing out" (I Timothy 6:7).

However, the previous balance sheet may be complete to the banker, but it is incomplete. To have a complete and accurate balance sheet of John Doe, we must include his spiritual assets, spiritual liabilities and spiritual owner's equity. To do this, first we must determine if John Doe is a believer or not. If John Doe is a believer, his balance sheet will be entirely different from his balance sheet as an unbeliever. The difference trust/faith in Jesus makes in a person's balance sheet is shown in the following examples.

JOHN DOE – THE UNBELIEVER BALANCE SHEET
(Day before his death)

Earthly Assets

Home............$	275,000
Stocks, 401k, etc.$	150,000
Cash.............$	1,500
Savings.......... $	7,000
Autos............ .$	30,000
Home Content.... $	15,000
Personal Items $	7,500

Total Earthly Assets **$486,000**

Earthly Liabilities & Owner's Equity

Liabilities:
Home Mortgage..........$170,000
Credit Cards.............$ 9,500
Student Loan...........$ 20,500
Auto Loans..............$ 20,000

Total Liabilities $220,000

Owner's Equity..............$266,000
(Remember: Equity is Assets less Liabilities)

Total Earthly Liabilities Owner's Equity **$486,000**

The above earthly portion of this Balance Sheet is the same he submitted to the bank for his loan.
Now, we must add the spiritual portion to his Balance Sheet.

Spiritual Assets

Eternal Death
Separation from God
Condemnation
Everlasting Punishment

Spiritual Liabilities

Sin

Spiritual Equity
-0-

Some Scripture must be taken into consideration to understand the above. "The wages of sin is death" (Romans 6:23). Here, death means spiritual death – separation from God. Also, if a person never believes/trusts in Jesus, he is condemned (John 3:18) and "shall be punished with everlasting destruction" (II Thessalonians 1:9a). These aforementioned Scriptures are some of his spiritual assets. How he got his assets, according to Scripture, is that "all have sinned" (Romans 3:23). Sin is his spiritual liability. Allow me to repeat, assets are what he has. He has these assets because of the spiritual liability of sin. John Doe's Spiritual Equity is zero. "For by grace are ye saved through faith; and that not of yourselves: it is the gift of God: not of works, lest any man should boast" (Ephesians 2:8-9 KJV). He has done nothing (-0-) to accept the gift of God. He never placed his trust in Christ, therefore, his spiritual assets – eternal death, separation from God, condemnation, everlasting punishment, etc. remain on his account while living here on earth.

Therefore, John Doe, the unbeliever, would have the above complete and accurate balance sheet which will include his financial and spiritual assets, liabilities and equity.

John Doe, the believer, will have a different looking balance sheet.

JOHN DOE – THE BELIEVER BALANCE SHEET
(Day before his death)

Earthly Assets

Home.............$	275,000
Stocks, 401k, etc.$	150,000
Cash...............$	1,500
Savings........... $	7,000
Autos.............$	30,000
Home Content.... $	15,000
Personal Items $	7,500

Total Earthly Assets — $ 486,000

Earthly Liabilities & Owner's Equity

Liabilities:

Home Mortgage........$170,000
Credit Cards............$ 9,500
Student Loan.......... ..$ 20,500
Auto Loans..............$ 20,000

Total Liabilities — $220,000

Owner's Equity........... $266,000

Total Earthly Liabilities & Owner's Equity..........$486,000

The above earthly portion of this Balance Sheet is the same he submitted to the bank for his loan.

Spiritual Assets

Eternal Death
Separation from God
Condemnation   ****All Cancelled****
Everlasting Punishment
Forgiveness of sin Eph. 1: 6-7
Eternal Life John 3:15
No Condemnation Romans 8:1
All of the promises of God

Spiritual Liabilities

Sin

All Cancelled

Spiritual Equity

Trust/Belief in Jesus

Remember, Assets is what you have and liabilities and equity is how you got the assets.

When John Doe placed his trust/belief in Jesus, God forgave/cancelled his sins.

> You were dead because of your sins and because your sinful nature was not yet cut away. Then God made you alive with Christ, for he forgave all our sins. He canceled the record of the charges against us and took it away by nailing it to the cross (Colossians 2:13-14 NLT).
>
> So we praise God for the glorious grace he has poured out on us who belong to his dear Son. He is so rich in kindness and grace that he purchased our freedom with the blood of his Son and forgave our sins (Ephesians 1:6-7 NLT).

With the forgiveness (cancelation) of sin, his spiritual assets – eternal death, separation from God, condemnation, and eternal punishment are no longer on the balance sheet of John Doe the believer. Remember, the liability of sin is how he got those spiritual assets. But this is only a part of what took place when John Doe trusted/believed in Jesus. Sin and the penalty of sin were not only cancelled, but John Doe received much more. For example:

The Holy Spirit – "And when you believed in Christ, he identified you as his own by giving you the Holy Spirit, whom he promised long ago. The Spirit is God's guarantee that he will give us the inheritance he promised and that he has purchased us to be his own people. He did this so we would praise and glorify him" (Ephesians 1:13b-14 NLT).

Eternal Life – "whoever believes in Him [Jesus] should not perish but have eternal life" (John 3:15).

No condemnation – "There is therefore now no condemnation to those who are in Christ Jesus" (Romans 8:1b).

In addition, according to Scripture, atonement, substitution, righteousness, adoption, reconciliation, justification, sanctification, security, resurrection, glorification and all the other promises of God were added to John Doe's balance sheet. My purpose is not to get into an in-depth discussion of various doctrines, but simply to show that John Doe and all believers get every promise made by God when they trust in Jesus. All of these additions are accounted to John Doe's Balance Sheet because "God presented Jesus as the sacrifice for sin. People are made right with God when they believe that Jesus sacrificed his life, shedding his blood" (Romans 3: 25a NLT). "The blood of Jesus Christ His Son cleanses us from all sin" (I John1:7b).

The two balance sheets above represent John Doe as an unbeliever and John Doe as a believer <u>before he dies</u>. When he dies, both balance sheets will change. The date of the "Death Day Balance Sheet" is unknown but it is coming. There is a time for each of us to die. "A time to be born, and a time to die" (Ecclesiastes 3:2a). "It is appointed unto men once to die, but after this the judgment" (Hebrews 9:27 KJV). Death is certain. All the earthly assets, liabilities and owner's equity cannot go beyond death's door and will become zeros on the believer's and the unbeliever's balance sheet at death. We own nothing. "For we brought nothing into this world, and it is certain we can carry nothing out" (I Timothy 6:7). The spiritual assets, spiritual liabilities and spiritual owner's equity will continue to exist.

On the day he dies, John Doe will either be a believer or an unbeliever. Those are the only two possibilities – not only for John Doe but for everyone. First, we will look at the "Balance Sheet" of John Doe the unbeliever on the day of his death.

JOHN DOE (The Unbeliever) BALANCE SHEET
(Date of his death)

ASSETS

Eternal Death   Romans 6:23
Separation from God II Thes. 1: 8-9
Condemnation   Romans 5:18
Everlasting Punishment   II Thes. 1: 8-9

LIABILITIES
Sin

OWNER'S EQUITY
-0-

As we look at the above balance sheet, remember that assets are what he has and liabilities and owner's equity is how he got those assets. Because John Doe never believed/trusted in Jesus as his Savior, his debt of sin was never taken care of on earth. Therefore, John Doe will experience eternal death, separation from God, condemnation and everlasting punishment.

The "Balance Sheet" of John Doe the believer on the day of his death is completely different. The reason it is so different is that John Doe trusted/believed in Jesus. His trust/belief in Jesus while on earth *did* go beyond death's door. As result, all the promises of God follow that trust and his balance sheet would be the following:

JOHN DOE (The Believer) BALANCE SHEET
(Date of his death)

ASSETS   **LIABILITIES**
Forgiveness of sin   Eph 1:6-7   -0-
Eternal Life   John 3:15
No Condemnation   Romans 8: 1
Glorified Body   Philippians 3: 20-21   **OWNER'S EQUITY**
Heaven   John 14: 1-4   Trust/Belief in Jesus
All of the promises of God

By looking at the balance sheets above, it would be apparent that John Doe, the believer, has a lot to look forward to and John Doe, the unbeliever, has damnation ahead. Again, let me say, these are the only two types of Death Day Balance Sheets that a person can have. Every person on earth will have one or the other.

You

If today is your "Death Day," which balance sheet would you have – the believer's or the unbeliever's? The balance sheet for the unbeliever and the balance sheet for the believer are eternally and totally different. The reason for the difference is faith in Jesus. Does your balance sheet have "Trust/Belief in Jesus" on it? Jesus wants to be on your balance sheet. "And this is the will of Him who sent Me, that everyone who sees the Son and believes in Him may have everlasting life; and I will raise him up at the last day" (John 6:40). "The Lord is not slack concerning His promise, as some count slackness, but is longsuffering toward us, not willing that any should perish, but that all should come to repentance" (II Peter 3:9). Not only does He want to be on your balance sheet, He has given us simple accounting instructions on how to put "Trust/Belief in Jesus" on your balance sheet.

> That if you confess with your mouth the Lord
> Jesus and believe in your heart that God has
> raised Him from the dead, you will be saved.
> For with the heart one believes unto
> righteousness, and with the mouth confession
> is made unto salvation...For "whoever calls on
> the name of the LORD shall be saved" (Romans
> 10:9-10,13).

Accounting, Jesus and You. "So then every one of us shall give account of himself [everyone will have a balance sheet to present] to God" (Romans 14:12).

Chapter 19: Why, Jesus and You

"Look not mournfully into the past; it comes not back. Wisely improve the future."[1]

Why

As a boy raised in the country, I would have chores to do. Most of those chores I would put off. Now don't get me wrong, "obedience" was not just a word at our house. I understood very well that there were consequences for disobedience, but I still tried to delay the work. Maybe I just thought a few minutes wouldn't matter. Maybe it was laziness. Whatever it was, the disobedience was corrected. There were also times when my mom would tell me to do something, and not thinking, I would say, "Why?" Most of the time I knew why, but the word seemed to just jump out of my mouth. Wrong response! I can hear her now, "Because I told you so." The "why" that I asked as a child was answered quickly and with an answer that I easily understood.

Now that I look back on those times, I realize the chores were not as bad as I thought. And my mom's replies were great lessons of responsibility, respect, and authority. Nowadays, it would be nice to have some of that energy that allowed me to do the chores. Also, with my mom in heaven, "because I told you so" is remembered with great affection.

My problem is not the "why" of the past. My problem is the "why" of the present. I realize it may be possible that some Christians have never asked "why." Evidently, I am not as strong as those believers because I have used the word "why" many times in my Christian life. Often, the "why" that I ask today doesn't receive a fast response nor an answer that I understand. As a matter of fact, sometimes it seems I receive no answer at all.

As a child or as an adult, we learn by asking questions. The word "why" is a tool for learning. As a child, I would frequently ask "why" and learn from the answer. But as an adult, I have often cried out "why" not to learn, but cried out "why" in agony. It would seem there was no way an answer was possible, and therefore nothing to learn. There was no way anyone could answer my "why" in a way that I could understand.

Now the statement above may give some doubts about my faith in Christ. If it does, let me assure you that is not the case. As the old hymn, "The Solid Rock" proclaims,

> My hope is built on nothing less than Jesus blood and righteousness. I dare not trust the sweetest frame, but wholly lean on Jesus name. On Christ the solid rock I stand, all other ground is sinking sand. All other ground is sinking sand.[2]

God wants us to be honest and cry out to Him. As Christians, we seem to think we should keep it all bottled up inside and should never ask why. What will other Christians think? Do we have such little faith? It seems many people don't want to express in words what God already knows is in our hearts. David often poured out his thoughts and emotions to God. He was honest with God. Robert S. McGee in his excellent book *The Search for Significance* made the following observation.

> Many of us mistakenly believe that God doesn't want us to be honest about our lives. We think that He will be upset with us if we tell Him how we really feel. But the Scriptures tell us that God does not want us to be superficial – in our relationship with Him, with others, or in our own lives. David wrote, *Surely you desire truth in the inner parts; you teach me wisdom in the inmost place* (Psalm 51:6 NIV).
>
> The Lord desires truth and honesty at the deepest level, and wants us to experience His love, forgiveness, and power in all areas of our lives. Experiencing His love does not mean that all of our thoughts, emotions, and behaviors will be pleasant and pure. It means that we can be *real*, feeling pain and joy, love and anger, confidence and confusion.[3]

With that said, I do want to be honest about my "whys" which have been cries of agony. Most of those "whys" were directed at God. The old question of "why do bad things happen to good people" has been addressed by hundreds, if not thousands of people. Nevertheless, when you are right in the middle of those "bad things," those books, sermons, tracts and personal conversations provide very little help. Maybe the following personal example, testimony, or confession will help clarify my "whys" that I have cried out.

The business world had been very good to me, but I never had absolute fulfillment in it. There was always another deal, another sale, or another goal to meet. My days were occupied with laboring "for what does not satisfy" (Isaiah 55:2). At the same time, I was active in my local church, teaching Sunday school, serving as a deacon and occasionally speaking at various churches. Looking back, my service may have been nothing more than trying to avoid obedience. Then a string of events, too much to cover here, caused me to take a good hard look at my priorities in my life. The conclusion was apparent, changes had to be made. I realized all of this was not just a mental conclusion but a calling that had been suppressed for years by profit and loss. As a result, I enrolled in seminary at the age of 44. With a degree in accounting and years of experience in business, I soon realized I didn't understand all the "holy" language of theology.

After graduation, I served bi-vocationally as the minister of education at First Baptist Church of Moody. I cannot express the joy that Donna and I had serving there. We loved the people and knew God had placed us there. In my mind this was perfect. I could manage a business and serve at the church, but God had a different plan. Obedient to His call, I left the business and starting serving full time as minister of education at Eden Westside Baptist Church. An old friend, Jacky Connell, was pastor, and the people received us with love. The Lord had blessed, but after four years, God was about to move us to another area of service.

I received a phone call from a member of Heritage Baptist in Pell City. Over the years, I had taught a couple of Bible studies at the church and thought the call could be to discuss teaching another study. That was not the case. The purpose of the meeting was to ask me to consider serving as pastor of the church. I was surprised to say the least. I could think of a million reasons not to accept. I asked for time to pray and seek

God's will in the matter. This was one of the hardest decisions that I have ever made. The church had lost membership and was down to a few people. My concern was not the number of people, but me. In my mind it was apparent that this assembly needed a very experienced pastor. I had no experience as a pastor. However, I was well aware that the Lord had declared, "For My thoughts are not your thoughts, nor are your ways My ways" (Isaiah 55:8).

Finally, after about a month of trying to rationalize why someone else would be better, our prayers were answered, and I knew the call was from God. I wanted to be obedient to serve in the place where He had appointed. I had come to realize that I could be there for two months, two years, twenty years or whatever amount of time, but that was in His hands. I accepted the call to serve as pastor. To say that I was concerned would be a huge understatement. I knew I was going into waters that I had never been in before. I certainly could have used the prayer of A. W. Tozer when he prayed:

> Lord, we're inundated today with "big preachers." And while we appreciate their gifts and ministries, I pray today for all who are "little preachers." Help them not to be discouraged by their seeming smallness but to be faithful servant of Yours, declaring with great passion the message of the Book, in the power of the Holy Spirit. Amen.[4]

The first year and a half, the Lord blessed in a mighty way. I was apprehensive about all the firsts: The first sermon, the first communion, the first business meeting and especially the first baptism. To prepare for the first baptism, Donna allowed me to practice using her as the candidate. After about three times, she assured me "if you don't have it right by now, you are never going to get it right." We look back with great fondness and joy on those first eighteen months. Little did we know what the coming years would bring.

In August of 2005, Donna was diagnosed with breast cancer. I will never forget the words when the doctor said to Donna: "You have breast cancer and it is the type that is very aggressive." I watched her suffer through chemotherapy and other horrors of cancer. At that time, I didn't understand why. "Why?! We are trying to do our best serving You. Why?" In February of 2006, Donna received her last chemo treatment, but the healing process continued. We continued to serve at Heritage and God continued to bless. God healed Donna and she continues to be by my side. We give God the glory. However, I still don't know the answer to "why."

The following years were not uneventful. During that time, part of my index finger had to be amputated. My mom's health continued to decline with Alzheimer's. Donna and my mom had to have pacemakers installed within two weeks of each other. I had to have major back surgery. Our youngest son and his wife moved out of state. Donna's dad passed away unexpectedly. My mom, who was living with us, had to be placed in an Alzheimer's assisted living facility. With all this going on, I was still trying to pastor. Donna, my wife, my best friend, my encourager and my heart, labored more than I. I can definitely tell you, I asked "why?" Why all the "bad things" when we are trying to serve the Lord? Why?!!! Even through all that, God continued to bless, but He gave no answer to "why."

In addition, in July 2009, tragedy struck our family. I will never forget discovering my brother-in-law and sister-in-law had been murdered. The loss was devastating. For over three years, all the legal mess that came with the tragedy continued to open the wound again and again. Finally, almost three years from the crime, the trial date was set. Little did we know my mom would be going on to be with the Lord the day before the trial was to begin. The second day of the trial required testimony from me. That night, the visitation service for friends was at the funeral home. The next day while the trial continued, my mom's funeral service was held.

Donna and I have asked "Why?" We have screamed "Why!!" Instead of an answer, Donna was given a verse that she shared with me:

> Be merciful to me, O God, be merciful to me! For my soul trusts in You; And in the shadow of Your wings I will make my refuge, Until these calamities have passed by (Psalm 57:1).

Donna wrote this verse on notes and stuck them everywhere in the house. The verse became a song that I couldn't get out of my head. I have no musical training. All those lines and notes above and below the words of a song mean nothing to me. Nevertheless, the words of Psalm 57:1 became a song for me. I could sing it to myself. I continued to write the words that came to my heart. They helped me express my feelings within and to God. The song/poem ended up like this:

In the Shadow of His Wings

In the shadow of His wings, I'll find my refuge there
In the shadow of His wings, I'll find His love and care

When the darkness of the days seem to never go away
I'll find shelter in the shadow of His wings

The days all begin with loneliness as my friend
But he is no friend who steals the joy within

All the questions of why – seem to never, never die

As the sun begins to sink, my mind begins to think
Of the restless night ahead, of the memories in my head

The night is filled with prayer – as I lie there in despair
Am I being shunned? Where is the Holy One?

The day begins with stares – I just sit – I really don't care

So I bow my head again and talk to my Friend
He knows where I have been and I ask Him to end
The agony within and the attacks the enemy sends

Instead a still small voice – reminds me of a choice

I chose to believe the promises are true and He will get me
through

Then a song comes to me – a simple melody
It confirms my security and the love He has for me

That is why I'll praise my King and to Him will I sing

In the shadow of His wings I found my refuge there
In the shadow of His wings I found His love and care

The darkness will go away – there will be brighter days
Because I'm sheltered in the shadow of His wings

Please don't misinterpret the purpose of mentioning all

these incidents and emotions. It is not for sympathy. There are persecuted Christians and missionaries around the world that suffer much, much worse on a day to day basis. It is not difficult to find individuals in our own community, country, and the world that are going through much worse. All you have to do is read articles from *The Voice of the Martyrs* or *Samaritans Purse* or other wonderful organizations that reaches out to those in need. Better yet, visit a local children's hospital.

My purpose is to tell you of my personal experiences and how those experiences have caused me to ask "why" a lot of times. "Why" was screamed out in agony. Meanwhile, God continued to bless – not only at church, but in so many ways. Over the years, God has been very good to me. Sure, I could make a list of "bad things" that has happened, but I could make a much longer list of the "good things" that has happened to me – all undeserved.

"Why do bad things happen to good people?" I doubt if anyone can give an adequate answer to a person that is in the middle of "bad things." But I do believe that we should be honest with God about them. We should scream out "why" and not try to cover our real feelings within. We ask, "Why do bad things happen to good people?" when deep down inside, we are saying, "God, why do you let bad things happen to good people?" Then I am reminded of what Jesus said, "No one is good but One, that is, God" (Matthew 19:17b).

Crying out to God and asking "why" is nothing new. In the Old Testament, we find the book of Habakkuk. In the first verse, Habakkuk is identified as a prophet. When we think of a prophet, we think of someone who is "close to God," "who has got it all together," or "who has a great amount of faith." But in Habakkuk we find a prophet who is asking questions. He does not understand. He is crying out "why?" Notice some of the questions, he is asking God.

How long, LORD, must I call for help, but you do not listen? Or cry out to you, "Violence!" but you do not save? Why do you make me look at injustice? Why do you tolerate wrongdoing? Destruction and violence are before me; there is strife, and conflict abounds (Habakkuk 1:2-3 NIV).

Habakkuk is asking God, "Why don't You do something?" Habakkuk wants God to tell him why He doesn't stop the pain, violence, injustice, and suffering of the righteousness at the hands of the wicked. God gives Habakkuk an answer, but it is not the answer that Habakkuk wants to hear. As a result, Habakkuk asks more questions.

God, you're from eternity, aren't you?
Holy God, we aren't going to die, are we?
God, you chose Babylonians for your judgment work?
Rock-Solid God, you gave them the job of discipline?
But you can't be serious!
You can't condone evil!
So why don't you do something about this?
Why are you silent now?
This outrage!
Evil men swallow up the righteous and you stand around and watch!
You're treating men and women as so many fish in the ocean,
Swimming without direction, swimming but not getting anywhere.
Then this evil Babylonian arrives and goes fishing.
He pulls in a good catch.

He catches his limit and fills his creel—
a good day of fishing! He's happy!
He praises his rod and reel,
piles his fishing gear on an altar and worships it!
It's made his day, and he's going to eat well tonight!
Are you going to let this go on and on?
Will you let this Babylonian fisherman
Fish like a weekend angler, killing people as if
they're nothing but fish?
(Habakkuk 1:12-17 MSG).

Habakkuk is saying what a lot of Christians avoid saying. They may think it but are afraid God will be mad or disappointed with them if they speak it. Let me say this before I continue. If God is going to get mad, it will be caused by what is in our hearts not what is in our mouths. What comes from the mouth has birth in the heart. Concerning disappointment, how can God be disappointed? Webster defines disappoint as "to fail to come up to the expectation or hope of."[5] If God is omniscient – and He is – He knows everything – past, present and future. If He already knows what someone is thinking and what they are going to do, then how can a person disappoint Him? Habakkuk is asking "why?" Habakkuk's questions should encourage us to do the same. Be honest with God. We should not be afraid to ask questions of God. Phillip Yancey in his thought provoking book *Disappointment With God* made the following observation about Job:

> One bold message in the Book of Job is that you can say anything to God. Throw at him your grief, your anger, your doubt, your bitterness, your betrayal, your disappointment—he can absorb them all...God can

193

deal with every human response save one. He cannot abide the response I fall back on instinctively: an attempt to ignore him or treat him as though he does not exist.[6]

Whether you are a preacher, a doctor, a missionary, a mechanic, a nurse, a mother, a father, or whatever label you have, it makes no difference and gives you no exemption from asking "why?" But, one thing is certain. If you are a Christian, you will have "bad things" happen to you and just like many of the saints in the Bible, you will cry out "why??!!"

It is easy for us to understand how we can cry out "why," but have you ever thought about God saying "why?"

Jesus

A great title for a book would be *When God Asked Why*. There may be one now. It is the truth. Jesus also asked "why."

> Now from the sixth hour until the ninth hour there was darkness over all the land. And about the ninth hour Jesus cried out with a loud voice, saying, "Eli, Eli, lama sabachthani?" that is, "My God, My God, why have You forsaken Me?" (Matthew 27:45-46).

I believe the "why" that Jesus asked on the cross was so agonizing and painful that no human being can ever understand. Notice that "Jesus cried with a loud voice." Jesus did not whisper this cry to God the Father. He said it with a loud voice. "Why" is not a complex word that requires a Ph.D. to understand. *Barnes Notes – Notes on the New Testament* adds:

194

This expression is one denoting intense suffering. It has been difficult to understand in what sense Jesus was forsaken by God. It is certain that God approved his work. It is certain that he was innocent. He had done nothing to forfeit the favor of God. As his own Son – holy, harmless, undefiled, and obedient – God still loved him.[7]

With the above comments in mind, a new question may come to our mind. In addition to asking why do bad things happen to good people, we may ask, "Why did bad things happen to God?" The answer may be that what we perceive as bad is not always bad. We may be looking at the situation from an earthly view rather than a heavenly view. "For now we see through a glass, darkly; but then face to face: now I know in part; but then shall I know even as also I am known" (I Corinthians 13:12 KJV). From an earthly point of view, Jesus suffered extremely bad things at Calvary. But from a heavenly view, it was the greatest thing that has ever happened for mankind.

One thing is for certain. God is sovereign. He has not and will not ever make a mistake. Our problem is we can only see from our earthly perspective.

Over the years, I have heard and read many good reasons "why" bad things happen. None really gave me the answer that allowed me to completely understand. That would be impossible because if I understood why God allows bad things to happen to good people, I would be God and that definitely is not true. Therefore, I will take what I learned a long time ago and apply it to my life now. "Why?" The answer is "because He told me so."

Again, let me quote the inspired insight of Phillip Yancey from his book *Disappointment With God*:

Not until history has run its course will we understand how "all things work together for good." Faith means believing in advance what will only make sense in reverse."[8]

No one is exempt from tragedy or disappointment – God himself was not exempt. Jesus offered no immunity, no way out of the unfairness, but rather a way through it to the other side...The Cross of Christ may have overcome evil, but it did not overcome unfairness. For that, Easter is required.[9]

The three-day pattern – tragedy, darkness, triumph – became for New Testament writers a template that can be applied to all our times of testing. We can look back on Jesus, the proof of God's love, even though we may never get an answer to our "Why?" questions. Good Friday demonstrates that God has not abandoned us to our pain. The evils and sufferings that afflict our lives are so real and so significant to God that he willed to share them and endure them himself. He too is "acquainted with grief." On that day, Jesus himself experienced the silence of God – it was Psalm 22, not Psalm 23 that he quoted from the cross.

And Easter Sunday shows that, in the end, suffering will not triumph.[10]

You

The purpose of this chapter is not to reveal some new truth as to why bad things happen to good people. Instead, it is to encourage you to be honest and cry out to Him from the very depth of your heart. Jesus understands. We may not understand it now, but we will. I hope the following illustration will help.

The famous artist Thomas Nast once sought to explain the mystery of sorrow. With rapid strokes of his brushes he painted a beautiful country scene on a canvas—green meadows, fields ripe with grain, a house and barn, a rippling brook, birds in the trees, and a bright, blue sky with fleecy clouds. He stepped back from the easel, and the audience applauded loudly. It was a wonderful, peaceful scene.

"But," he said, "the picture is not finished," and turned to brush it with dark, somber colors. Sweeping the canvas with apparent recklessness, he made daubs and blotches such as a child might make in smearing. Out went the blue sky and peaceful countryside until only a patch of each was left at the top and bottom. "Now," he said, "the picture is finished and perfect." No one applauded. All sat puzzled and doubtful.

Then the artist turned the picture on one end, and the whole crowd gasped in amazement, for now they saw a beautiful, dark waterfall, masses of water pouring over moss-covered rocks and raising rainbow hues in the air. He had changed the first quiet scene into the rich, beautiful second one while the audience thought he was ruining the canvas.[11]

If you are going into, through, or out of "bad things," I pray a verse or a song will be placed in your heart that assures you that God is with you. Although you may feel you are the canvas and the Great Artist is making a mistake, He is not. One day you will see the finished picture. Meanwhile, it would be good for us to remember:

> When God needs a person for His service – a good person, an effective person, a humble person – why does He most often turn to a person in deep trouble? Why does He seek out a person deep in the crucible of suffering, a person who is not the jovial, "happy-happy" kind? I can only say that this is the way of God with His human creation.[12]

Why, Jesus and You. Why? Maybe people need other people that can relate to them. Maybe empathy is needed a lot more than sympathy.

> Belgian Father Damien, on the Hawaiian island of Molokai, contracted leprosy, but God kept him alive for 16 long years for the sole purpose of preaching to others similarly afflicted. [13]

Maybe your "bad thing" has prepared you to be a Father Damien. If that is the case, ask God to place in your life a person that needs your understanding, love, and encouragement. Someone who is hurting is waiting on you.

Chapter 20: The Mantle

"Let all that I am praise the LORD."
(Psalm 103:22)

The Mantle

As I wrote this final chapter, I began to think of all the other stories and personal experiences that were not included in this book. Basically, the chapters were a few of the "Jesus and You" sermons that I had preached over the years – causing me to have many fond memories of some church services. However, the memories were not limited just to church. It was memories of years gone by in general.

I guess it is just the natural thing to do as we get older – to think of the past more often. After all, I certainly have more years behind me than ahead. There is definitely nothing sad about that statement. It is just a matter of fact. It happens to all of us.

Now before you start ordering flowers and getting ready for a funeral, I pray the Lord gives Donna and me many, many, many more years to enjoy and serve Him and enjoy the next two generations – our sons and their families. Yet, there have been certain occurrences in my life over the past few years that have made me think of the past and the future.

For example, this Thanksgiving was the first Thanksgiving that Donna and I celebrated without one of our parents being alive. This is not the first time this has happened to anyone, but it was the first time for us.

After Thanksgiving, I realized with my mom going on to be with the Lord, the "mantle" had been passed. When I say "mantle," I am referring to what happened in I Kings 19. Before Elijah went to heaven, the Lord told Elijah to anoint Elisha to succeed him as prophet. Obeying God, Elijah put his "mantle" (cloak) around Elisha. This confirmed that Elisha was going on to be with the Lord, and Elisha was to become Elijah's successor.

Since neither Donna nor I have any living siblings, the passing of the mantle was a natural life process, not a selection or appointment process. There was no physical mantle that was thrown around me, but the transfer of the mantle was made.

The mantle that I received from my mom was in excellent condition. The mantle fabric was 100 percent Matthew 22:37-38. She loved the Lord her God with all her being, and she loved her neighbor as much as she did herself. In addition, the fabric was woven in such a manner that revealed the two verses in every area of her life.

With cancer and Alzheimer's, her last few years had not been easy, but she never complained. As a matter of fact, I can never remember her complaining about anything. It seemed, she could find good in everything and reminded us all of how thankful we should be.

Although, she only had a sixth grade education, she taught with wisdom and in unique ways. For example, if you had a flat tire and were late for work that was a reason to thank God and recognize His sovereignty. It should not be a time of frustration. God had simply delayed your trip in order to protect you from an accident you could have been in if you were on time.

Her mantle had so many stories woven into it. Stories about the family, The Great Depression, World War II, her small school, the animals she loved, and so much more.

Her priorities were the opposite of today's society. Her treasures were her relationship to God, her family, and her love and concern for other people. She cared very little about earthly "treasures." After her death, we found several Christmas gifts stuck in the back of a drawer and notes and cards in more guarded places.

She would always say "thank you" even to a nurse that had given her a shot. She had no fear of death and looked forward to being with the Lord and her loved ones who had gone on before her. She mentioned some by name those last few days.

During the last few hours of her life, Donna was on her left side holding her hand, and I was on the right side holding her hand. I thank God we were there. No crying out with pain, no struggle. She went out of this world as she lived it – by the grace of God. In the middle of the day as we held her hands, her breathing slowed gradually and then stopped – she had gone on to be with the Lord.

The mantle was passed.

However, since the mantle was passed, I began to wonder about the mantle that will be passed on to Joey Jr. and Matt. What kind of condition will it be in?

The fabric will be the same – 100 percent Matthew 22:37-38. Donna and I both believe and try to live this everyday of our lives. Hopefully, Joey and Matt have seen Donna and I grow in our love for each other and the Lord. We have not been perfect. We have failed in many areas, but God has blessed in spite of our failures. Also, I believe the mantle will have the same fabric for generations to come because Joey Jr.

and Emily, and Matt and Sarah are Christians. Also, I am confident their children will be great Christian leaders and servants of the true and living God.

Nevertheless, my concern is not the fabric, but how the fabric is woven to reveal Matthew 22:37-38 in every area of my life.

It will be impossible to pass on the exact mantle that I received from my mom because all the stories and life experiences woven into that mantle were from my mom's life. The mantle that I will pass on to Joey Jr. and Matt will have my experiences and stories, and hopefully, some of my mom's.

I hope they see woven in the fabric of the Matthew 22:37-38 mantle, the importance of family and some of the experiences I had as a child: The Sunday afternoons at Grandma and Granddaddy Rich's with the made from scratch banana pudding that was created in a dish pan, the water bucket and dipper on the back porch, the saw dust pile, the corn cob fights, the catfish heads nailed to a pine tree where Granddaddy had cleaned some catfish, and so much more.

The deep-rooted love of the rural areas and the great appreciation of God's creation – a beautiful water fall and a view of five or six mountain ridges –both unknown by so many and so close to home, the sound of frogs singing their song on the summer nights, the owl in the early evening, the full moon shining on the frost, the stars shining so bright without the competition of electric lights, the hawk gliding through the air effortlessly, the blue birds gathering food for their young, the beauty of each season, especially the spring when the earth cries out, " He is alive," was ingrained in me and will be a part of the mantle that I pass on.

If the mantle being 100 percent Matthew 22:37-38 is woven in a manner that reveals these verses in my life, I will be content to pass the mantle on.

I hope after reading *Walmart, Jesus and You,* you will begin to discover the Gospel of Jesus Christ in everyday living. But the only way that is possible is to trust/believe in Jesus as your personal Savior. Then as the Holy Spirit abides in you, He will open your eyes to see things as He sees them. Maybe that was what Joyce Kilmer saw when he wrote the poem "Trees."

Trees

I think that I shall never see
A poem lovely as a tree.

A tree whose hungry mouth is prest
Against the earth's sweet flowing breast;

A tree that looks at God all day,
And lifts her leafy arms to pray;

A tree that may in Summer wear
A nest of robins in her hair;

Upon whose bosom snow has lain;
Who intimately lives with rain.

Poems are made by fools like me,
But only God can make a tree.

What condition is your mantle that you will be passing to the next generation?

Scripture Index

Proverbs
12:19   *Forked Tongue, Jesus and You*
22:6   *Forked Tongue, Jesus and You*
27:1   *Fingers, Jesus, and You*

Ecclesiastes
8:7   *Fingers, Jesus and You*

Isaiah
41:10   *Elvis, Jesus and You*
55:8   *Why, Jesus and You*
55:8-9   *Electronics, Jesus and You*

Jeremiah
22:13-14, 18a, 23   *Walmart, Jesus and You*
22:19   *Walmart, Jesus and You*
29:11   *Walmart, Jesus and You*

Ezekiel
18:20   *Parents, Jesus and You*

Habakkuk
1:2-3   *Why, Jesus and You*
1:12-17   *Why, Jesus and You*

Matthew
1:21,23b   *Electronics, Jesus and You*
2:11   *Memories, Jesus and You*
2:13   *Memories, Jesus and You*
2:14   *Memories, Jesus and You*
5:13-16   *Aunt Nell, Jochebed, Jesus and You*
11:28   *Buzzards, Jesus and You*
12:24   *Forked Tongue, Jesus and You*
13:1-2   *Junk, Jesus and You*
16:21-22   *Fingers, Jesus and You*
17:27   *Memories, Jesus and You*
21:15   *Children, Jesus and You*
23:23-24   *Buzzards, Jesus and You*
23:37   *Mothers, Jesus and You*
24:27   *Fingers, Jesus and You*
24:37-39   *Fingers, Jesus and You*

24:44	*Fingers, Jesus and You*
25:31-32	*Forked Tongue, Jesus and You*
25:35-36,40	*Memories, Jesus and You*
26:33-35	*Lewers St., Jesus and You*
26:63-64a	*Electronics, Jesus and You*
26:59-60	*Forked Tongue, Jesus and You*
26:63-65	*Forked Tongue, Jesus and You*
27:41-42	*Forked Tongue, Jesus and You*
27:45-46	*Why, Jesus and You*
27:62-64	*Forked Tongue, Jesus and You*
28:19-20	*Opportunities, Jesus and You*

Mark

8:31	*TV, Movies, Jesus and You*
14:61-64	*Combo#2, Jesus and You*

Luke

2:19	*Memories, Jesus and You*
12:8-9	*Electronics, Jesus and You*
12:15b -20	*Elvis, Jesus and You*
22:41-42	*TV, Movies, Jesus and You*
23:34	*Computers, Jesus and You*
23:40-43	*Parents, Jesus and You*
24:10-11	*Opportunities, Jesus and You*

John

3:15	*Forked Tongue, Jesus and You*
3:15	*Accounting, Jesus and You*
3:16-17	*Mothers, Jesus and You*
3:16-18	*Electronics, Jesus and You*
3:36	*Computers, Jesus and You*
4:10	*Children, Jesus and You*
4::26	*Electronics, Jesus and You*
4:28-29	*Children, Jesus and You*
5:24	*Combo #2, Jesus and You*
6:26	*Children, Jesus and You*
6:38	*Electronics, Jesus and You*
6:40	*Accounting, Jesus and You*
6:69	*Electronics, Jesus and You*
8:43-45	*Forked Tongue, Jesus and You*
8:58	*Electronics, Jesus and You*

9:6	*Junk, Jesus and You*
10:30	*Electronics, Jesus and You*
11:40	*Electronics, Jesus and You*
14:2b-3	*Electronics, Jesus and You*
14:4-6	*Electronics, Jesus and You*
16:1-4a	*TV, Jesus and You*
16:33	*TV, Jesus and You*
19:26-27	*Mothers, Jesus and You*
21:25	*Memories, Jesus and You*

Acts

7:22	*Aunt Nell, Jochebed, Jesus and You*
8:36	*Junk, Jesus and You*
9:1-2	*Lewers St., Jesus and You*
9:3-9	*Lewers St., Jesus and You*
9:6	*Lewers St., Jesus and You*
9:10-16a	*Lewers St., Jesus and You*
9:14	*Lewers St., Jesus and You*
12:1-11	*Junk, Jesus and You*
16:25-27	*Elvis, Jesus and You*
16:29-34	*Elvis, Jesus and You*

Romans

2:11	*Opportunities, Jesus and You*
5:9	*Computers, Jesus and You*
6:23	*Computers, Jesus and You*
10:9	*Computers, Jesus and You*
10:9-10,13	*Accounting, Jesus and You*
14:12	*Parents, Jesus and You*

I Corinthians

10:31	*Children, Jesus and You*
10:31	*Lewers St., Jesus and You*
13:12	*Why, Jesus and You*
15:1-4	*Fingers, Jesus and You*
15:4-7	*Electronics, Jesus and You*

II Corinthians

11:23-28	*Lewers St., Jesus and You*

Galatians
6:5   *Parents, Jesus and You*

Ephesians
1: 6-7   *Accounting, Jesus and You*
1:13-14   *Accounting, Jesus and You*
2:8-9   *Accounting, Jesus and You*

Philippians
3:10   *TV, Jesus and You*
4:11b-13   *Elvis, Jesus and You*

Colossians
2:13-14   *Accounting, Jesus and You*

I Thessalonians
1:10   *Computers, Jesus and You*

II Thessalonians
1:8b-9   *Electronics, Jesus and You*

__I Timothy__
6:7   *Accounting, Jesus and You*

Hebrews
9:27   *Accounting, Jesus and You*
11:24-25   *Aunt Nell, Jochebed, Jesus and You*
13:5-6   *Elvis, Jesus and You*

James
4:14   *Elvis, Jesus and You*

I Peter
5:11   *Lewers St., Jesus and You*

II Peter
3:9   *Accounting, Jesus and You*

I John
1:9   *Computers, Jesus and You*

End Notes

Ch. 1

[1] Compiled by Dennis J. Hester, The Vance Havner Quotebook, (Grand Rapids: Baker Book House, 1986), 23.

[2] Compiled by Alice Gray, *More Stories for the Heart* (Oregon: Multnomah Publishers, Inc., 1997), 275-276

Ch. 2

[1] Compiled by Ronald Eggert, Tozer on Christian Leadership (Pennsylvania: Christian Publications, Inc., 2001), September 10

[2] Compiled by Ronald Eggert, *Tozer on Christian Leadership*, October 28

[3] Craig Brian Larson and Leadership Journal, 750 Engaging Illustrations for Preachers, Teachers and Writers (Michigan: Baker Book House, 1993), 423, Illustration # 529

[4] Compiled by Ronald Eggert, *Tozer on Christian Leadership*, August 14

[5] Compiled by Dennis J. Hester, *The Vance Havner Quotebook* (Grand Rapids: Baker Book House, 1986), 109.

Ch. 3

[1] Vern MClellan,The Complete Book of Practical Proverbs & Wacky Wit (Wheaton, Ilinois: Tyndale House Publishers, Inc., 1996), 54, quote by Yogi Berra

[2] Donald Grey Barnhouse, *Let Me Illustrarte* (Grand Rapids: Fleming H. Revell, division Baker Book House, 1967), 246-247.

[3] Compiled by Ronald Eggert, *Tozer on Christian Leadership,* December 21

Ch. 4

[1] Joe Taylor Ford, Sourcebook of Wit and Wisdom (Canton, Ohio: Communication Resources, Inc., 1996), 157

[2] Herschel H. Hobbs & Ronald K Brown, Complier, My Favorite Illustrations (Nashville: Broadman Press, 1990), 78

[3] Elon Foster, 6000 Sermon Illustrations,1974 Reprint (Grand Rapids: Baker Book House, 1992), 89, #654

Ch. 5

[1] McLellan, The Complete Book of Practical Proverbs & Wacky Wit, 26
[2] Lowell D. Streiker, A Treasury of Humor (Massachusetts: Hendrickson Publishers, Inc., 2000), 104
[3] Craig Brian Larson and Leadership Journal, 750 Engaging Illustrations for Preachers, Teachers and Writers, 475, Illustration #589
[4] Harper Shannon, Riches in Romans (Nashville: Broadman Press, 1969), 15
[5] Walter A. Elwell, Editor Abridged by Peter Toon, The Concise Evangelical Dictionary of Theology (Grand Rapids: Baker Book House, 1991), 565
[6] Ibid., 468

Ch. 6

[1] Charles R. Swindoll, Swindoll's Ultimate Book of Illustrations & Quotes (Nashville: Thomas Nelson Publishers, 1998), 119
[2] Swindoll, Swindoll's Ultimate Book of Illustrations & Quotes, 437
[3] Webster's Seventh New Collegiate dictionary (Massachusetts: G. & C. Merriam Company, Publishers, 1967) USA defines 'contented'
[4] Perfect Illustrations for Every Topic and Occcasion, Content with God's Gifts – pg. 48-49 from –compiled by the editors of PreachingToday.com (Illinois: Tyndale House Publishers Inc., 2002 Christianity Today International)
[5] Craig Brian Larson and Leadership Journal, 750 Engaging Illustrations for Preachers, Teachers and Writers, 341, Illustration 425
[6] C.S. Lewis, A Year with C. S. Lewis –Daily readings from His Classic Works – Edited by Patricia S. Klein, April 15 (New York: Harper Collins Publishers, 2003), 117
[7] Swindoll, Swindoll's Ultimate Book of Illustrations & Quotes, 437
[8] Compiled by Ronald Eggert, Tozer on Christian Leadership, October 17

Ch. 7

[1] McLellan, The Complete Book of Practical Proverbs & Wacky Wit, 164
[2] Craig Brian Larson and Leadership Journal, 750 Engaging Illustrations for Preachers, Teachers and Writers, 363, illustration #452
[3] Ibid., 165
[4] Ibid.
[5] Ibid.
[6] Ibid.
[7] Foster, 6000 Sermon Illustrations, 463, illustration #4036
[8] Albert Barnes, Notes on the New Testament- The Gospels Volume , 1949.

Reprint. Edited by Robert Frew, Book of John (Grand Rapids: Baker Book House, 2005), 192

[9] Ibid., 372

[10] Compiled by David F. Burgess, Encyclopedia of Sermon Illustrations (The Concordia Publishing House, 1988), 53-54, Illustration 205

Ch. 8

[1] McLellan, The Complete Book of Practical Proverbs & Wacky Wit, 174

[2] Swindoll, Swindoll's Ultimate Book of Illustrations & Quotes, 389

[3] Compiled by David F. Burgess, Encyclopedia of Sermon Illustration, 150, Illustration # 690

[4] David Jeremiah, Life Wide Open – (Tennessee: Integrity Publishers, a division of Integrity Media, Inc., 2003), 91

[5] Joe Taylor Ford, Sourcebook of Wit and Wisdom (Ohio: Communication Resources, Inc. 1996), 230

[6] Foster, 6000 Sermon Illustrations, 484, #4245

[7] Hobbs, Ronald K Brown, Complier, My Favorite Illustrations, 90

Ch. 9

[1] Joe Taylor Ford, Sourcebook of Wit and Wisdom, 63a

[2] Compiled by Ronald Eggert, Tozer on Christian Leadership, December 24

[3] Warren W. Wiersbe, The Bible Exposition Commentary, Vol.1, Matthew-Galations (Illinois: Victor Books-Division of Scripture Press, 1989), 97

[4] Compiled by Ronald Eggert, Tozer on Christian Leadership, December 18

Ch. 10

[1] Joe Taylor Ford, Sourcebook of Wit and Wisdom, 104

[2] Bruce Wilkinson, The Three Chairs – Experiencing Spiritual Breakthroughs – Member Study Guide (Nashville: LifeWay Press, 1999),11

[3] Ibid., 11

[4] Ibid., 12

[5] Compiled by David F. Burgess, Encyclopedia of Sermon Illustrations, 134, Illustration # 615

Ch. 11

[1] Joe Taylor Ford, Sourcebook of Wit and Wisdom, 82b – Rabindranath Tagore

[2] Dr. Anthony P Witham as quoted in God's Little Instruction Book for Dad (Tulsa: Honor Books, 1994), 21

[3] Hobbs, My Favorite Illustrations, 99

[4] Joe Taylor Ford, Sourcebook of Wit and Wisdom, 76, Leon Yankwich quote
[5] Gigi Graham Tchividjian as quoted God's Little Instruction Book for Dad,127
[6] Joe Taylor Ford, Sourcebook of Wit and Wisdom, 79, Ralph Waldo Emerson quote
[7] Ibid., 79
[8] Perfect Illustrations for Every Topic and Occasion – Compiled by the editors of Preaching Today.com, 35, Frailties of Speech, citation: Rick Eshbaugh
[9] Cal and Rose Samra, More Holy Humor (1997) Fellowship of Merry Christians, Inc. Guideposts, Carmel, New York. Published by special arrangement with Thomas Nelson Publishers, 40
[10] Oswald Chambers, My Utmost For His Highest – (Ohio: Barbor & Company, Copyright renewed 1963, Grand Rapids: Discovery House Publishers),72
[11] Ibid., 118
[12] Compiled by Ronald Eggert, Tozer on Christian Leadership, April 15

Ch. 12
[1] McLellan, The Complete Book of Practical Proverbs & Wacky Wit, 215, Henry Adams quote
[2] Foster, 6000 Sermon Illustrations, 380, #3281, Spurgeon quote
[3] Foster, 6000 Sermon Illustrations, 381 #3283 , W.M. Punshon quote

Ch. 13
[1] McLellan, The Complete Book of Practical Proverbs & Wacky Wit, 90
[2] Bruce Barton, D.Min., Philip Comfort, Ph.D., Grant Osborne, Ph. D., Linda K. Taylor, Dave Veerman, M.Div., Life Application New Testament Commentary (Wheaton: Tyndale House Publishers, Inc., 2001), 207
[3] Ibid., 207
[4] Swindoll, Swindoll's Ultimate Book of Illustrations & Quotes, 383 quoted by John Greenleaf Whittier
[5] Compiled by Ronald Eggert, Tozer on Christian Leadership, August 16

Ch. 14
[1] John A Garraty, The American Nation (New York: Harper & Row Publishers, 1966), 478
[2] Ibid., 477
[3] The World of the American Indian (Washington, D.C.: National Geographic Society, 1974), 315
[4] Ibid., 326
[5] Ibid.

[6] Ibid.

[7] Garraty, The American Nation, 457

[8] The World of the American Indian, 330

[9] Garraty, The American Nation, 481

[10] Swindoll, Swindoll's Ultimate Book of Illustrations & Quotes, 344

[11] Hobbs, My Favorite Illustrations, 140

Ch. 16

[1] Joe Taylor Ford, Sourcebook of Wit and Wisdom, 205

[2] Henrietta C. Mears, What The Bible Is All About (Glendale: Regal Books, Div. of Gospel Light Publications, 1966), 1

[3] Westminister Shorter Catechism-1647

[4] Bruce Barton, D.Min., Philip Comfort, Ph.D., Grant Osborne, Ph. D., Linda K. Taylor, Dave Veerman, M.Div., Life Application New Testament Commentary, 435

[5] J. Vernon McGee, Thru the Bible with J. Vernon McGee, Vol. 4 (Nashville: Thomas Nelson, Inc., 1983), 478

[6] Decision Magazine – April 2012-Special Issue—published by The Billy Graham Evangelistic Association, Charlotte, NC 2012 Pg 5

Ch. 17

[1] McLellan The Complete Book of Practical Proverbs & Wacky Wit, 182 John Locke quote

[2] Hobbs, My Favorite Illustrations, 100

[3] Compiled by David F. Burgess, Encyclopedia of Sermon Illustrations, 183, Illustration # 847

Ch. 19

[1] Herbert V. Prochnow, Treasury of Inspiration (Grand Rapids: Baker Book House, 1958), 112

[2] "The Solid Rock" (1863) words and music by William Bradbury based on Edward Mote's "My Hope is Built on Nothing Less" (1834)

[3] Robert S. McGee, Search for Significance, 2nd ed. (Texas: Rapha Publishing,1990), 5

[4] Compiled by Ronald Eggert, Tozer on Christian Leadership, May 5

[5] Webster's Seventh New Collegiate Dictionary USA defines 'disappoint' (Springfield, Massachusetts: G. & C. Merriam Company, 1967)

[6] Philip Yancey, Disappointment with God (Grand Rapids: Zondervan Publishing House, 1988), 235 disappointed

[7] Barnes, Notes on the New Testament, 312, Matthew 27:46

[8] Philip Yancey, Disappointment with God, 201

[9] Ibid., 186

[10] Ibid., 211-212

[11] Complied by David F. Burgess, Encyclopedia of Sermon Illustrations, 189-190, Ref # 885 – The Mystery of Sorrow

[12] Compiled by Ronald Eggert, Tozer on Christian Leadership, Dec. 10

18307159R00117

Made in the USA
Charleston, SC
27 March 2013